Wakefield Press

Geoff Brock

Greg Mayfield, an award-winning journalist with the *Recorder*, lives in Port Pirie with his wife Ros, a breast-care nurse. Their son Louis is senior journalist at the *Whyalla News*.

GEOFF BROCK

THE MAN WHO SAVED A CITY

Greg Mayfield

Wakefield Press

Wakefield Press
16 Rose Street
Mile End
South Australia 5031
www.wakefieldpress.com.au

First published 2018

Copyright © Greg Mayfield, 2018

All rights reserved. This book is copyright. Apart from any fair dealing for the purposes of private study, research, criticism or review, as permitted under the Copyright Act, no part may be reproduced without written permission. Enquiries should be addressed to the publisher.

Edited by Julia Beaven, Wakefield Press
Typeset by Michael Deves, Wakefield Press

The author thanks Fairfax Media for permission to use photographs and material in the text.

ISBN 978 1 74305 522 9

A catalogue record for this book is available from the National Library of Australia

For

Ros, Louis and Ruth

Contents

APPENDICES

Foreword

I am now a good friend of Geoff Brock's. We didn't grow up together or work together, but for many years I have admired and respected him. One should respect your mayor, or local member of parliament. I was taught to respect from a young age, but Geoff has earned this respect. His passion for our community and for what he thinks will improve it is unsurpassed, as it is for other communities he represents in his most recent roles as Regional Development Minister and Local Government Minister.

Geoff is a working-class man, happy to get his hands dirty for a cause he believes in. You see him regularly bailed up listening to issues his many friends and acquaintances might want to discuss. Some of these people he has never met before, but they soon become friends. Although some issues might seem trivial, Geoff will always listen and help where he can. I seriously don't know how he fits it all in, and still has time for his beautiful family.

Another great asset is Geoff's positive attitude. If it seems like a good idea and the community will benefit, then Geoff will have a go. He likes to be liked – don't we all? – but he won't let his mates down. Like me, he sometimes struggles to find the right words to explain himself, but no one can question his desire. He also doesn't like to miss out. If something good is going on, Geoff wants to be a part of it. Not to cut the ribbon, but to help.

Although I have voted Liberal most of my life, I now vote for Geoff Brock, a politician who works best for our community. I wish there were more like him, politicians with the passion and the will to work hard for what they believe in.

Mark Hanlon
President, Port Pirie Chamber of Commerce and Industry, 2018

Chapter 1
A World of Difference

The rabbit-trapper's son from the Mid North of South Australia was on the phone to Zurich, Switzerland. Geoff Brock listened intently as a multi-billion-dollar metals company made its case for financial support. As the Independent candidate for the seat of Frome, based around Port Pirie, he knew that the phone conversation with Nyrstar's Michael Morley was a deal-breaker. It was March 2014 and Mr Brock had risen to become one of the political kingmakers of South Australia.

Geoff Brock grew up in a poor family at Wandearah, south of Port Pirie, in the 1950s, helping his father Ian with his livelihood of trapping and dressing rabbits for sale. The enterprise exposed the young Geoff to the realities of the commercial world for the first time. Now, many years later, he was helping to determine the fate of one of the world's biggest metal-processing companies and owner of the Port Pirie smelter.

The backdrop to the discussion with Mr Morley was the South Australian election, contested on 15 March 2014. The Labor Party held 23 seats, Liberals 22; 24 were needed to form government. The result hung on a knife-edge and the eyes of the nation were on Geoff Brock, along with fellow Independent for Fisher, Dr Bob Such. Both were to be asked to take on the role of kingmaker.

Geoff was now in a unique position to achieve something great for his home city and its major business, the Nyrstar lead and zinc smelter, his former employer. The lead smelter had been operating in Port Pirie for 120 years and was the most polluting site in all of the Nyrstar conglomerate's worldwide operations.

His telephone contact with Mr Morley came about as a result of Nyrstar's proposed $660 million upgrade of the Port Pirie site. This ambitious upgrade was to transform the smelter into a poly-metallic plant with the capacity to conduct 'urban mining' or extraction of metals from mobile phones, computers and televisions. At the same time, lead emissions would be dramatically cut, providing a better future for the children of Port Pirie, including Geoff's grandchildren.

The smelter, with its long-term future then in doubt, would be given a new lease of life if the 'transformation' went ahead. But there was a problem. The Tony Abbott-led Federal Government of Australia had already been approached about supporting the venture. The fiery Mr Abbott had taken his troops into a federal election in September 2013. About this time there had been simmering concerns about the level of federal financial support provided to companies such as the SPC fruit cannery in Victoria and Holden in South Australia.

Mr Abbott had defeated Labor's Kevin Rudd to take office, but there was no word on the backing that was so desperately needed by Nyrstar. Geoff Brock, who had been the Independent Member for his electorate since 2009, was by this time recovering from prostate cancer. The resilient parliamentarian was again out and about in his electorate, doing his work representing the voters. He prefers not describe his work in his electorate as 'campaigning' because it is something he does year-round, not necessarily with an election in mind. But the reality was voters would go to the polls in South Australia and he was everywhere.

'Some people were saying that I would go to the opening of a postage stamp,' he said.

> *I was diagnosed with prostate cancer 10 to 12 months before the election. You start to question whether you are going to live or not. At one stage I was given six months to live because of the way the doctor was reading the data. Then I was told it was not as bad as it was thought, but I needed a prostatectomy.*

Geoff defied the doctors to throw himself back into the fray two weeks after surgery, instead of taking the regulation six weeks' total rest.

'The story was going around that I was dying of cancer, anyway,' he said. 'I was active in the electorate, and campaigned for office, but I never went door-knocking or holding street-corner meetings.' He visited Tarlee, Riverton, the Clare Valley, Bute, Port Broughton and surrounding townships, and was prominent in his home town.

He faced challenges at the poll from the Liberal candidate Kendall Jackson and Labor's Marcus Connelly. The late Mr Connelly was the nephew of the late Ted Connelly, a former Port Pirie mayor, who in 1975 held the balance of power in the State Parliament as the Independent Member for Pirie. At that time, Ted Connelly cast his vote with the Don Dunstan-led Labor Party to form a minority government. Completing his transformation, he later rejoined the Labor Party.

Port Pirie was waiting with bated breath to see what Geoff Brock would do in similar circumstances. As far as pre-polling assessments for the 2014 election were concerned, the sitting member simply calculated that he had about a 30 per cent chance of success as one of three contenders.

On 15 March, he cast his vote at the Hannan Street Baptist Church polling place. After visiting the 29 other polling places across the electorate, he returned home to be confronted by a television satellite dish on his front lawn and swarms of cameras and media representatives. After a series of interviews, he retreated inside his house to flick on the television to see the 7 pm news bulletin; it looked like he would retain his seat. Supporters and local identities gathered at the house to celebrate. Finally, at 1.30 am, he and partner Lyn Akker retired to bed.

About 6 am next day, while clearing up the debris from the party, he had a phone call from Jay Weatherill, who had led Labor to the polls as sitting premier. Geoff was bemused. 'The polls had indicated a Liberal win and I was thinking, *What do I say to this man?*'

What Mr Weatherill had to say shocked him. The Labor leader needed to talk because the seat tally was locked at 23 to Labor and 22 to the Liberals. The Liberals could take office if both Mr Brock and Dr Such threw their weight behind the right-wing party instead of the left-leaning Mr Weatherill. But, conversely, one or both of them could choose to support Mr Weatherill to form government.

Geoff Brock has never been a member of a political party, but could see the negatives that would flow from a period of uncertainty surrounding the future of the incoming administration, pending the pair's decisions. In no time, Geoff Brock was dressed in his business clothes for a Sunday meeting in Adelaide with Mr Weatherill.

In the meantime, he was contacted by Liberal leader Steven Marshall, who said he also wanted to discuss electoral prospects with Geoff and Dr Such.

'I was happy to support a party to form a stable government,' Geoff Brock recalled.

> *The adrenalin was flowing pretty freely and my mind was all over the place. I was trying to understand how a person such as myself came to be in this situation.*
>
> *I consider myself an ordinary person. As my working career developed, I had been a manager based at Port Augusta for BP Australia covering the biggest territory in the world. I worked my way up with Nyrstar through manual jobs including being on the jackhammer and pumping out septic tanks. I never envisaged this happening in my wildest dreams.*

As negotiations kicked off, he met Dr Such at the old Treasury Building in Adelaide where again there was the glare and blare of publicity. Both men had been speaking with the two party leaders, but they were never in the same room at the same time during these machinations. Taking a team approach, the two Independents arranged another private meeting in the cafeteria of Parliament House. Geoff Brock was enjoying roast beef when a television camera was aggressively placed on the table beside him by hovering media crews. Pressure was rising at a time when both men were acutely aware of their role in history.

As a condition of their support for a new government, Dr Such wanted parliamentary reform and Geoff wanted an amazing 57 concessions for residents of his electorate. Three days had elapsed since the election and Geoff was growing weary of the constant media barrage. He longed to return to the simple days of being the Independent Member for Frome.

He spoke to Lyn who urged him to make a decision. She said Dr

Such had been in parliament for 25 years compared with Geoff's five years and he should seek guidance from him.

'I was the country boy, inexperienced, and I struggled,' Geoff Brock said.

Unexpectedly, his confidant and would-be mentor Dr Such, who had been pushing him to the fore at media conferences, then disappeared from the public stage. Confused and suddenly alone, Geoff Brock returned to Port Pirie to host a meeting at his electorate office with the mayors and chief executive officers of the five local government councils in his district: Barunga West District Council, Northern Areas Council, Clare and Gilbert Valleys Council, Wakefield Regional Council and Port Pirie Regional Council. The aim was to discuss concessions to be sought in return for his vote on the floor of parliament.

A pact was struck to seek a range of benefits. Despite attempts at confidentiality, his plans soon leaked to the media. Nevertheless, Geoff Brock put his list to both leaders before it became known that Dr Such was embroiled in a health crisis.

On the Saturday after the election, Dr Such announced he was suffering from brain cancer and publicly sought three months' leave of absence from his duties as a parliamentarian. Within hours, Mr

Weatherill reacted to the emergency and was on the line to the Port Pirie-based politician, saying he was heading to the northern city to discuss forming government. If Geoff Brock rejected Mr Weatherill's overtures and sided with the Liberals, there would be a 23–23 tie without Dr Such's vote. This would force the Governor to appoint a minority government or to install a caretaker government pending fresh elections.

'It might have suited the major parties, but it would not have suited the minor parties or independents to go to a fresh poll because of the extra cost involved,' Geoff said. 'There would be uncertainty for business – could South Australia govern itself?'

As the drama unfolded, Geoff faced a simultaneous challenge from overseas; Zurich was calling. In 2013, in the lead-up to the 2014 poll, Geoff Brock had held talks with Premier Weatherill and Treasurer Tom Koutsantonis about the need for financial support for Nyrstar.

'No government was going to give them a bailout,' the Independent politician said.

The Federal Labor government's carbon tax was costing the smelter $10 to $15 million a year. We talked about the proposed new plant in Port Pirie to produce lower emissions and lower blood-lead levels in children and ensure the future of the works for Port Pirie and the surrounding areas.

The original plant had been there for 120 years and it had gone through voluntary administration in the past. We talked about how as a nation we could facilitate that transformation and work with the Commonwealth government to achieve this.

The uncertainty was affecting 2500 to 3000 people directly and indirectly employed by the smelter. It was hanging over the head of South Australia's first provincial city.

When the election was called these discussions were ongoing. First up in my discussions with Mr Weatherill and Liberal leader Steven Marshall was consideration of the smelters – the need for a commitment for loans or underwriting or other financial support. But Mr Abbott's federal government was not making a definite commitment.

As the days ticked over after the state election, Geoff Brock took a series of international phone calls at his seafront unit in Adelaide. The calls came at 2 am or 3 am, amid the crashing of waves on the shore. On the line was Michael Morley, a senior executive of Nyrstar, speaking from the company's head office in the Swiss capital. Nystar had notified the European Stock Exchange of its plans for the transformation in Port Pirie, and needed a loan guarantee to help with the project.

'The whole project may have fallen over if they breached the time-frame for the underwriting,' Geoff Brock said.

In the phone calls, Michael Morley asked Geoff to say who would govern South Australia – and, in reality, who would have the power to grant Geoff's concession for Port Pirie in the form of a $291 million underwriting of the project. The pressure was becoming almost unbearable.

Geoff Brock recalled:

> *They were fairly long conversations. I would go out to the balcony. I could hear the ocean and I could see the moon on the water and smell the sea. It was a nice environment in which to have a discussion, but the discussion was not relaxing. I was thinking about my family and friends in Port Pirie and the future of the smelter for the next 50 years. If we didn't get this right and the smelter closed, that would have been a real blow to this city.*
>
> *We had been promised so many things over the years and this community had never had something come to fruition.*

Mr Morley had flown to Adelaide twice to meet Geoff Brock at the home of Bespoke political lobbyist Ian Smith. No one else knew the Nyrstar executive was in town as they chatted over a barbecue and wine.

It was now a week after the election and Labor leader Jay Weatherill decided to travel to Port Pirie to try one last time to win Geoff's backing for a minority government. He arrived at the local man's house at 11 am; there was work to do, and, as the day lengthened into evening, pizza to eat. Soon after Mr Weatherill's arrival, Geoff had a phone call from his daughter to question the unmarked security car, aerials protruding, parked beside his house. Mr Weatherill quickly dispatched the car from the scene – no one was to know he was involved in discussions to shape the future of the state.

'There was only one way to go,' said Geoff, 'a minority, stable government. I had to think of the reputation of the state and its ability to govern. There was a three-month window with the European Stock Exchange for the underwriting to be confirmed. I went out to get a pizza for Jay.

As the group munched on fast food at Geoff's house, Mr Weatherill's chief of staff Simon Blewett, a two-finger typist, laboriously set out the terms of the agreement – and the concessions – for the seat of Frome in return for its representative agreeing to vote Labor into power.

Mr Weatherill and Mr Brock had had two close escapes from the media during their incognito late-night dealings. The senior journalist with the local newspaper the *Recorder* lives a few doors from Geoff's house. He had a phone call from a source who suggested that Jay Weatherill was in town and at the Frome parliamentarian's house. The journalist drove past the house, didn't spot a government car and decided against knocking on the door.

The second brush with publicity came when one of Mr Weatherill's staff members, Jarrad Pilkington, was walking in the main street of the city that night and was confronted by two radio journalists. His comment that he just happened to be in town satisfied their curiosity.

Mr Weatherill's final visit resulted in a pizza shop owner winning national publicity and having bragging rights for his crusty product. It also left a major employer with a half-billion-dollar premier project. To cement the deal, the Labor leader handed over a letter outlining the terms of the agreement between the incoming government and Geoff Brock. It stated that if the federal government failed to support the city with underwriting for Nyrstar, then the Labor Party would step in to commit to the $291 million loan guarantee.

Later, Geoff Brock announced to the media that he had won the agreement and the smelter could survive. In response, Liberal figures suggested that the federal Abbott government no longer had an obligation to support the project because the South Australian Labor Party had already done so. Geoff Brock thought South Australian Liberal leader Steven Marshall would have mirrored the commitment, but this was not to be.

On the Sunday after Jay Weatherill's whirlwind visit to Port Pirie, Geoff Brock and his partner Lyn woke early for a drive to Adelaide where the agreement between himself and the Labor Party was to be unveiled.

We stopped once at Port Wakefield, but I made 14 pit stops on the road to answer calls of nature. My nerves were absolutely shot and my bladder was working overtime. I had never been to the State Administration Centre where the announcement was going to take place.

It was cloak-and-dagger, like James Bond's secret service. I was ushered through a rear door and taken to the 15th floor.

With formalities unfolding, he shook the new premier's hand before asking, 'Where's the toilet?'

In the days after the historic agreement, Nyrstar's Michael Morley communicated to Geoff the relief that he and the company's board felt at the outcome of the negotiations. But despite the lofty heights to which Mr Brock had risen, he was not immune from abuse and threatening phone calls in the aftermath of his decision.

He refrained from celebrating the outcome until after the 'transformation' agreement papers were signed at a ceremony at the smelter involving Cabinet ministers and Mr Morley. Standing to one side of the podium, Geoff Brock became emotional and misty-eyed. His acquaintance, lobbyist Ian Smith, turned and said to him: 'Are you okay? You're not a real politician, are you?'

After months of tortuous negotiation, pushing for the best for the people of Port Pirie and region and dealing with powerbrokers at the highest level, Geoff Brock replied, somewhat ironically, 'No.'

Chapter 2
Living off the Land

The fierce outback sun was beating down on the jockey-sized frame of 13-year-old Geoff Brock. It had been wearying work, as always, harvesting rabbits from the land with his father Ian. Taking a respite from the backbreaking task, the young Geoff stood on the shores of a vast, brackish lake filled with bore water. It was bathtime at Frome Downs, in the north of South Australia. Like other rabbit trappers scattered around the rich pickings of the Downs, the family of Ian Brock was living off the land. Their caravan was perched under a mulga tree on top of a sand dune.

After raising a sweat helping his father on the rounds, Geoff washed himself in the warm underground-sourced water of the lake. Little did he know that one day, living in Port Pirie, he would represent the namesake of the area by becoming the Member for Frome in the State Parliament.

The Brocks had come to be in Frome Downs after an adventurous and near-penniless journey from Frankston and Mildura, in Victoria, to the SA Riverland before heading to Redhill, Wandearah, and finally Port Pirie. In the 1940s, Ian Brock had returned from World War II service in New Guinea to work as a taxi driver in Frankston, a beachside suburb of Melbourne. He had developed a lung infection during his tour of duty and had a condition similar to asthma. Fearing for his health prospects, doctors told him to leave the moist air of Melbourne for a drier climate.

Ian considered his options and the possible impact on his wife Joan and 18-month-old son Geoff, the first of seven children. Joan had been raised in an orphanage and had married Ian in her late teens. She worked in a nursing home before Geoff's birth.

Upon reaching the north-western Victorian city of Mildura, they rented an old farmhouse. Ian performed odd jobs and, through his contacts, developed an interest in rabbit trapping. News reached him of a rabbit plague interstate – ideal for his fledgling trade – and the family uprooted to spend about 18 months in the SA Riverland.

He bought more traps and boosted the family income from sales of dressed rabbits. This was fortunate because at the time unemployment benefits were meagre. With a caravan in tow, the family was soon on the move again, this time to Redhill, south of Port Pirie, where Ian rented a farmhouse and did odd jobs. After talking to a rabbit exporter in Melbourne, he arranged to supply the animals for shipment to Japan, a major step in his career. Ian took the family to Wandearah, closer to Port Pirie, where the rabbits were in huge numbers.

From their farmhouse on Old Broughton Road, Geoff, then aged four, would go out on the rounds with his father who would puff on a roll-your-own cigarette and keep conversation to a minimum lest they scared the rabbits. Geoff recalls:

> *The mobile freezer was the size of a semi-trailer. There was no electricity at the farmhouse so we had a 32-volt generator to power the chiller. It also powered the house. These chillers would hold about 3000 pairs of rabbits. A 'pair' was created*

when the hind leg of a dressed rabbit was slit and another carcass's hind leg slipped through it. They were then looped over a rail.

When we went out, we would set 200 to 300 traps. The rabbits were so thick that when you drove at sunset, you were running over them because they were just a mass. You would set your trap wherever they were travelling. You would put it in a hole and put the pin in the ground with the open jaws of the trap and trigger-plate. Fresh dirt was spread over the trigger-plate so the rabbit thought it was a fresh dung hill. They would come in there to fossick around and the trap would go off. The trap was attached to the pin embedded in the ground and the rabbit could not escape.

We would set the traps at 10 am, then again at dusk, again at 8 pm or 9 pm and again at 4 am or 5 am. You carried up to 20 of the rabbits in a hessian bag slung over your shoulder. Dad would drive the car and we kids would stand on the running boards beside the doors as he did his rounds. When we had been around to all the traps, we would return to the house to dress the rabbits for sale.

As an agent for export, Ian would accept carcasses from other trappers after first checking them for disease. Taking the Bedford tray truck, Ian and Geoff would travel to Baroota and Port Germein in search of more quarry in their 24-hour, seven-day-a-week job. The rabbits were so prolific that every trap set was producing a captured animal. It was a successful seven years for the family, but hard times were to follow.

By this time Geoff and his brother and sisters were attending

Pirie East Primary School, one classroom for students in Grades 1 to 7. Sometimes, he returned home to his parents to proudly show a sticker awarded to him for reading to the young children in the classroom as a 'Clayton's teacher'.

The family grew their own vegetables on the six-acre property and called at neighbouring farms to buy milk and cream. 'The milk was available fresh from the cow,' Geoff recalled. 'There was no pasteurisation and the milk came straight from the bucket. It was absolutely fantastic to come home to not only fresh milk, but also the cream. It had a magnificent taste that I remember very clearly.'

Life on the land was not always tough, it seems, and the Brocks found entertainment opportunities at nearby Port Pirie.

> *We would come into Port Pirie every Wednesday on the Bedford truck to the Shandon drive-in theatre's Ranch Night. They would screen cowboy movies such as* Hopalong Cassidy, The Cisco Kid *and* White Eagle. *There was a 'teaser' at the end of the show with the hero in peril and you had to come back the next week to see whether he survived. Dad would reverse the truck onto the viewing mound and we sat on seats on the tray on a summer's night with the speaker strategically located so we could hear every sound.*
>
> *For our entertainment, we also had the radio in the lounge room at home. We listened to serials such as the very funny* Greenbottle, *about a student's experiences as school. It was a great life.*

But nothing stays the same. Soon Geoff and his brothers and sisters were moved to Wandearah North Primary School then, when he was about 10 years old, with rabbits becoming more scarce, the family moved to Barry Street, Port Pirie, and he enrolled at Risdon Park Primary School.

'That was the biggest cultural shock of my life,' Geoff Brock said.

> *I came from a classroom with seven grades, one teacher and 20 students, to a classroom of about 30 students with numerous teachers. I was learning only Grade 7 material and was missing the interaction with the other grades that took place at my previous schools. It took me a while to adjust.*
>
> *Dad had given up rabbit trapping and was lugging wheat bags on the wharf. He carried the bags over his shoulder up the gangplank into the ship. It was a stevedoring operation and they called the numbers of the men to work each day. If they called your number, you worked; if not, you went home.*

As times got tougher, Ian had his spirits lifted by news that rabbits were again on the march in the north of the state. He bought a Fargo ute, loaded up the family's meagre belongings, hitched up the caravan and headed for another adventure.

When they reached Olary, there were reports of rabbits in the Frome Downs area. But the caravan snapped an axle. Country hospitality came to the fore when the group was rescued by the family living in the Frome homestead, who took them in and provided lunch, which they ate overlooking their flywire balcony as Ian and the stock hands welded up the axle.

Journeying on, they found a camping spot under a mulga tree on top of a sand dune. There was no running water. Illumination was from Tilley lamps and food was cooked on a Primus stove.

'We did things just as we had done at Wandearah,' Geoff said.

My brother Peter stayed with Mum at the camp and I went out with Dad. Dad was about six foot two inches tall and had receding brown hair, which he kept short. He carried a small knife in a pouch on his belt.

There was a supply truck driven by George F. Ding, who came every month to look after 20 or 30 trappers in the area. In our operation, we would set our traps in the spinifex and sand dunes. If there was a waterhole, we would put wire netting around it with a one-way gate so we could trap the rabbits inside. We got our water for the camp from an untapped bore that was boiling hot and flowed into a lake about a kilometre away. We put the water into drums and boiled it later to purify it. And we would bathe ourselves in the still-warm waters of the lake. There were thousands of gallons of water there.

The Brocks dined on braised rabbit, rabbit casserole and other rabbit dishes, but occasionally resorted to shooting a kangaroo if supplies of the other menu items became scarce. They enjoyed a barbecue hosted by stockmen mustering cattle in the area and invited the head rider Bill to their caravan for a meal of kangaroo.

This idyllic lifestyle, with the children being schooled by correspondence lessons, continued for 18 months, by which time Joan was pregnant with Lynda. With the impending birth, the family returned to Port Pirie where they rented a house, on Senate Road Extension, from Jeff Finlay, caretaker for Air BP at the airport. This, perhaps, was a taste of Geoff's future career with BP Australia, but for now the growing lad was embarking on difficult times.

Dad had no work, Mum was not working and we really started to fall on hard times. My brothers and sisters and I were wearing four-or-five-times hand-me-down clothes from the Salvation Army or opportunity shop. We had to walk to school at Risdon Park Primary in thongs because we didn't have shoes.

Dad later got a job as a porter at the hospital, but damaged his back while lifting a heavy patient and could not work there again. He then worked for the Commonwealth Railways on the East–West railway, travelling Port Pirie to Perth and return, leaving the family in Port Pirie for long periods.

By this time we were living in Barry Street, near our previous house, and Dad was supposed to send money back to us when he had it. A shop proprietor in Kingston Road allowed Mum to book up groceries and she would pay it off when Dad sent money. Unfortunately, there were times when there was no money and the store could not give more credit. So Mum sold our household furniture to raise cash to get provisions for the kids.

Geoff recalls his mother fondly.

It was a very trying time of our life, but I give credit to Mum because she always did her best. There would have been many occasions when she went to bed crying while trying to provide a better life for all of us. She was a proud woman. I remember lots of times there was no food . . . you went to the cupboard and there was nothing there. At other times we ate sausages and bread and dripping. We also mixed bread with warm milk for a filling meal. Mum could make something out of nothing.

She was petite and lovely and well groomed, and prepared to listen to any personal issues we had because Dad was not there a lot. She was particular about hygiene and cleanliness and if your hands were dirty, she would demand: 'Wash your hands with Solvol.' She was a great mum. She would have gone without things on many occasions to ensure we did not.

Developing into a teenager, Geoff did his best to set an example for his young siblings as a kind of male head of the family, but was soon called away. He joined his father on the West Coast of South Australia with the pair dossing down in disused farmhouses while tending the traps. 'We didn't have showers or baths. It made me appreciate how fortunate we are now,' Geoff said.

He recalled that during the family's hardships he was bullied at school because of the clothes he wore.

Quite often I would be ridiculed. I would be isolated. Sometimes we had no lunch to take to school. There were times at recess and lunchtime when I would have no one to talk to. I was bullied and often would get picked on and have a tussle. I never told my mother because, if you dobbed, you got worse the next day. I just took it in my stride. I am certainly not a fighter. I am a pacifist. I got picked on because I was smaller and called 'jockey'. After a while, it gives you an inferiority complex.

Asked how it now felt to have since become arguably Port Pirie's most popular man, he replied:

I have just been lucky. I suppose it has taught me that no matter who you are, whatever you are doing in life, everyone should be treated the same. I think I learned that at primary school, at Risdon Park in particular. It is not the cards you are dealt, but the way you play them. That is what I say to kids – if you want to do something, don't let anyone say you cannot do it.

The Brock clan comprised parents Ian and Joan, then, in order of age, Geoff, Peter, Mary, Ian, Keith, Lynda and Karyn. Ian died at the age of 77 in Port Pirie in April 1997 suffering from emphysema linked to his wartime health condition; Joan passed away aged 68 in December that year.

Ian had been a smoker, despite his indifferent health. He carried a packet of Capstan tobacco and a thin folder of cigarette papers with which to roll his own smokes.

'I can still see the bit of red ash, like a little furnace, at the end of the cigarette as the paper dangled from his lips,' Geoff Brock said.

Dad taught me pretty well to add and multiply numbers because he used to do it in his head when he was buying or selling rabbits. He instilled in me the importance of correct pronunciation and spelling; he would spell 'Constantinople' and I would have to repeat it and then spell it out.

But he was a tough father. If you did something wrong, you really got chastised . . . you got a belting.

Despite the ups-and-downs of his years spent outdoors, Geoff Brock thinks he has had a good life.

'If I died tomorrow, I have had a fortunate life,' he said. 'I have met a lot of people and done a lot more than I would have considered possible when I was trudging to the schoolyard in my thongs.'

Chapter 3

Dollars and Devotion

A yellow, illuminated ram sat on top of the Golden Fleece petrol bowser at the corner of Senate Road and Balmoral Road, Port Pirie. It was a beacon to a young man setting out on his first steps into employment. Geoff Brock had returned to Port Pirie after forays into rabbit trapping up north. He was a young man attending Intermediate classes at high school. His father, Ian, once again looking out for his son, had a chance conversation with Bob Voumard who ran the service station while Bob was filling the petrol tank of the Brock family car, a two-tone grey FJ Holden. Yes, Bob said, there was a vacancy for a driveway attendant at the garage.

After accepting the position, young Geoff rode his bicycle from the family's Housing Trust home in Barry Street to the garage to pump petrol and clean windscreens. His father and Bob Voumard had insisted he keep up his schooling while he worked on weekends.

> *I would be in the workshop cleaning up and as soon as I saw a car come in, I was out there, grabbing a squeegee, asking the driver what he wanted while I cleaned the windscreen. I always asked whether I could check under the bonnet. I would check the oil and water. We had to wipe down the bowsers to keep them clean and wipe the oil bottles because they would get condensation on them.*

Bob made sure we always had something to do, which has been a philosophy of mine ever since. He was always good to work for and was happy-go-lucky. He taught me about customer service and that when you did a job, you made sure you did it properly.

Geoff, aged 16, had finished his Intermediate Certificate when one day he called into the Four Square general store in Kingston Road, Port Pirie. It was run by Fred and Mary Wilson, who had supplied goods to his mother on credit in the family's time of need. By this time, he had his driver's licence and was once again in luck when he asked the Wilsons whether they had work for him at the shop.

He became a delivery boy, driving the store's white van with its long gearstick protruding from under the dashboard. It took all his concentration to change gears and steer the vehicle. Trips were made to the thriving Co-Operative Wholesalers Store, in York Road. The store was a hub for smaller shopkeepers to collect their goods from and deliver them to their outlets.

Geoff loaded the van with groceries and trundled back to Kingston Road in a series of trips during the week. He also took to the streets on his bicycle with a crate perched on the handlebars to deliver household items to residents.

'I took the box into the residence, unpacked the items for them and returned to the shop with the empty box,' Geoff recalled.

You were not allowed to accept tips. I met a lot of people. In summer they would ask whether I wanted a drink of cold lemonade and it was appreciated. It was a good transition stage for me, meeting so many people, considering how reserved I was at school.

It was not much money, but I loved the job. I was paid in pounds, shillings and pence. It was a start in life. I bought my first new clothes ever – a corduroy jacket and trousers – and had my photograph taken wearing them in the backyard.

Dad was still on the West Coast trapping rabbits and sending home money to Mum when he could. I gave money to Mum for board which helped her a little. I might have used the rest to buy cool drinks or lollies. At that stage, I didn't have a girlfriend.

With the advent of decimal currency in Australia in 1966, Geoff was soon paying dollars and cents to buy petrol for the family car. His father had asked him to keep his travel to a minimum, but 'mainies' – trips around the city centre streets with a load of passengers – were hard to resist. At times, Geoff would take mates from his street on rides through town.

His friends included John Power, later an academic at Flinders University; Cameron Coligan, who became a star Spencer Gulf League and SANFL footballer; and Sam Harris, who is a legendary local entertainer. Geoff's brother Peter would join them in the days before he left to join the army and sister Mary would sometimes come along for a spin.

Dad would tell me not to drive too far. So when I had the car, I would fill it up with a dollar's worth of petrol. Next day, when Dad got in the car, the petrol gauge would have not moved from its original position so I thought I was home free. But unknown to me, Dad was taking the odometer reading and realised that I had been driving around aimlessly.

The tight-knit neighbourhood around the trust home area soon produced a stroke of good fortune. Neville Flint, of the Commonwealth Employment Service, lived in nearby Plenty Street. He called into the Brock household to say that a job was available for a clerical officer with oil giant BP Australia at the then petroleum storage tanks in Solomontown, a suburb of Port Pirie. Was young Geoff interested in applying for the position?

The job interview was conducted by Jock Livingston, the father of one of Geoff's friends, John. Geoff, now 18, impressed his prospective employer and soon started on better money than he had received as a store delivery boy.

It was fitting that he should have his own transport to and from the tanks so he bought a black-grey Honda 90cc motorcycle from Brian Burgess at Union Motors, in Wandearah Road. After signing the ownership papers with his mother, his pride and joy – with numberplate TB-595 – was delivered to Barry Street. Geoff, having never ridden a motorcycle before, kick-started the engine and took off down the driveway – and into the picket fence between the houses nearby. He smashed several palings, but luckily the bike was undamaged, and he escaped with grazes. To this day he maintains that the throttle 'got caught'.

The motorcycle remained his mode of transport until, after saving some money, he spotted a hotted-up, blue FJ Holden at Union Motors. The car had been owned by Phil Fergusson, a panelbeater and motoring enthusiast, and featured a customised boot and tail-lights, a Ford four-on-the-floor transmission, lowered suspension, wide wheels, chrome exhaust and full-race camshaft.

'It went *hooomp . . . hooomp,*' Geoff said of the engine noise when the car was idling. 'It was a beautiful car. I thought I was king of the gang.' It was thirstier on petrol than the average Holden, but Geoff had a 15 per cent rebate on BP fuel, thanks to his job. Although he did plenty of 'mainies' in Port Pirie, the car was known to venture beyond the town limits.

One day, Geoff and his passengers, John Livingston, John Power and Darryl Baker, decided to travel to the BP Oasis service station, on the outskirts of the town. Someone then said, 'Let's go to Thompson's at Crystal Brook,' so they headed to the Mid North town with rock 'n' roll music blaring from the car radio. Once there, it was suggested that Port Wakefield should be the next destination . . . followed by a challenge to keep going to the Burger King at North Adelaide. A couple of hours later, the boys pulled up at the drive-through where the waitresses, wearing neat yellow uniforms, put a tray on the car window and delivered the final reward at journey's end: Burger King hamburgers all round.

Meanwhile, because of his career choice, he had the opportunity to earn extra income at local BP service stations at BP Ellen Street, run by Bob Smith, and BP Oasis run by Gerry Seed. As well, he worked the driveway at BP The Terrace, operated by John Thompson, and BP Balmoral, managed by Fred Fox. Geoff pumped petrol, performed grease-ups, changed tyres and cleaned the shelves. He served cheeseburgers and milkshakes in the cafeteria of the Oasis, then located in Warnertown Road, Bungama, until 1 am. With his regular employment and the part-time work, he was notching up paid hours on almost seven days of the week.

Wednesday was a night off when he attended parades as a

member of the Army Reserve at the old military headquarters on the corner of Mary Elie Street and The Terrace, now the TAFE campus. And Saturday night was devoted to recreational activities such as the Club 65 dances at the YMCA Hall, in Gertrude Street.

> *'That is when I met Arlene,' he said of his first encounter with his wife-to-be.*
>
> *Everyone had their different styles of dress and gangs, like the bodgies and widgies. You were real cool cats when you walked into these places.*
>
> *Arlene went to a different school, the Port Pirie Technical High School. She was a very vibrant person and everyone loved her. I was dancing with her in the style of the time, opposite each other in lines of boys and girls. I had a conversation with her, trying to chat her up. But the conversation was a bit one-sided. I could not understand her because of her strong Scottish accent.*
>
> *I jokingly said, 'Come back in two years' time when you can speak English,' and moved down the line to the next girl.*

About 18 months later, in 1967, Geoff was taking his lunchbreak from BP and called home to his mother's house for a bite to eat. Standing in the kitchen was Arlene Cabrie and her friend Dianne Ness. The Ness family had strong links with the Brocks because at one stage the four Brock boys were partnering the four Ness girls.

Geoff's mind was racing with recollections of the Club 65 encounter.

'Here was Arlene, the girl I had said should come back,' he said.

As fate would have it, Arlene's friend Dianne teamed up with Geoff's brother Peter. They have now been married for many years and have great-grandchildren. But what was to become of Arlene and Geoff?

Thanks to Geoff's 'guardian angel', his sister Mary, who intervened surreptitiously while also at home that day, a date was set for the blushing pair to go to a cabaret together. It almost fell through when Geoff was unable to fit in his suit. Geoff and Arlene instead went to the drive-in theatre, and held hands in Geoff's latest car, an immaculate brown-and-fawn HR Holden, which he greased every Sunday, painted its tyres black and polished the vinyl floors.

'If it was not for my sister Mary organising that first date, it might not have happened,' he said.

> *By now I could understand Arlene, this blue-eyed brunette with a lovely smile. We just seemed to hit it off. It was a smooth transition into a love story. We were having dinner at the Flinders Range Motor Inn in Port Pirie one Saturday night and Glenn and Ronnie Giles, from Port Germein, approached us and said they had just become engaged. They asked when we were going to do the same.*
>
> *From then onwards, everything fell into place. We got engaged when I was 21 and Arlene was 19. Everyone loved her. She was an apprentice hairdresser at a salon in York Road, but it was closing and her parents, Jack and Cathy Cabrie, bought the business so she could fulfil her apprenticeship.*
>
> *Arlene was born in Greenock, near Glasgow, in Scotland. Her dad came out to Australia as the pipe major in the Port Pirie Pipe Band and worked at the smelters as an electrician. When he was playing in the pipe band, he would wear a kilt.*

In 1989, Geoff took Arlene and their two children, Hayley and

Marisa, to Scotland, thanks to three X-Lotto wins of $1500, $2100 and $1400 and money earnt while working overtime.

'I have had lots of luck in my life,' he said.

While he and Arlene were courting, he moved to Adelaide with BP Australia, first boarding with his aunt, Violet Freane, in Lockleys. The young clerk had his own cottage at the rear of Aunt Violet's house. Later, he rented a two-bedroom flat about a kilometre away in Lockleys. In typical 1960s style, it was one of four apartments in a cream-brick block. Geoff would dine lavishly on the only meal that he could make in the kitchen – steak and mashed potato. Entertainment consisted of a watching television while sitting on a crate. An old card table with a couple of chairs was used for dining purposes.

The Adelaide–Port Pirie train service kept Geoff in touch with home. He would travel to see Arlene on Friday nights then stay the weekend until Sunday and catch the train back. Eventually, for more independence, he drove his car. The long kiss goodbye saw him leave Port Pirie on Sunday at progressively later departure times: 4 pm . . . then 6 pm . . . 9 pm . . . 10 pm . . . and finally 4 am on Monday, to travel straight to the office to start work bleary-eyed.

Geoff and Arlene were married on a sweltering summer's day on 3 February 1973 at the now-demolished white-walled Lutheran Church on the corner of Herbert Street and Senate Road in Port Pirie. Sweat was dripping off the groom and bride in 100-per cent humidity and century heat. Much-loved minister, the late Pastor Ern Heyne, conducted the ceremony. From time to time, he would turn away from the couple to wipe his face with a wet flannel.

'Pastor Heyne was a great man,' Geoff said.

Some of the things he did for us and for Mum when she was sick were outstanding. When I was about 14 years old I was thinking of becoming a missionary in New Guinea because he inspired me. Then I met Arlene so that went by the wayside.

After the wedding ceremony, about 140 guests gathered for the wedding reception at the popular Toledo Restaurant run by the Monogios family in Florence Street.

'I thanked everyone for coming and mentioned it was great that Arlene had to come all the way from Scotland to find a decent husband,' Mr Brock recalled. 'My Australian relatives applauded; the Scottish ones booed.'

Soon after, fate intervened and Mr and Mrs Brock were presented with the chance to move north to Port Augusta. The couple were faced with a make-or-break chance of a lifetime; would Geoff manage the northern part of the state for BP Australia? It was the company's biggest territory in the world. Trouble was, every other manager who had been to Port Augusta to do the job had divorced . . .

Chapter 4

From Outback to Ballot Box

All the desert sand in northern South Australia failed to halt Geoff Brock's march into the record books of BP Australia. He moved from Port Pirie to Port Augusta with new bride Arlene to manage Territory 336, which included Maree, Woomera, Coober Pedy, Ernabella Mission, Indulkana, Oodnadatta, Quorn and Hawker. It was nothing for him to travel for up to three weeks along remote tracks to service customers and roadhouses with orders for BP's petroleum products.

The story of one man's efforts to tame the vast unknown began one summer's day in Port Augusta. After he won the job, the Brocks were first put up at a motel, but later rented a house from Dudley Dighton who owned the motel. Arlene's mother Cathy would travel north from Port Pirie to keep her daughter company while Geoff was away on his outback runs.

The couple made many new friends and adopted South Augusta as their football club in the Spencer Gulf League after having barracked for Port Football Club back in Port Pirie. Arlene found work in her much-loved field of employment as a hairdresser at Kathy's Salon, a business owned by a Greek named Ulysses.

Buckling down to the task, Geoff at first set out on his journeys in an old Land Rover plagued by mechanical problems. He soon graduated to a Toyota Land Cruiser for safety reasons. It had long-range fuel tanks, four spare tyres, a refrigerated tucker box and two-way UHF radio linked to the flying doctor service in case of emergency.

He needed to be quick off the mark because the territory was the fastest growing district for the sale of fuel and lubricants.

'It was uncharted territory,' Geoff said. 'The mining operations were coming onstream and were boosting demand for our products.' Geoff's outstanding sales and distribution achievements were mentioned at company conferences.

It was a family-friendly company with golf tournaments, tenpin bowling events and social activities such as balls in Adelaide. Then it was back to the grind of up to 10 hours behind the wheel, watching spectacular sunrises over the saltpans near Kingoonya and mixing with the larrikins of the Coober Pedy and Andamooka opal fields.

'I have great memories of those places,' he said.

The outback hospitality was legendary. At the homesteads, they would invite you inside to have something to eat and drink. You had lots of time to think as you were driving. Your mind wanders. Sometimes I would leave the roads corrugated from the rain and go into the sand dunes for 15 kilometres to get back onto a better surface. There were wandering cattle, emus and kangaroos.

The company made a movie about our territory filmed at Quorn and Hawker – I would love to have a copy now. I can see them with the camera on a tripod. They started with Arlene giving me breakfast and then me giving her a kiss goodbye and me getting in the Land Cruiser. They screened the film at William Creek for about 400 people.

Geoff recalled one trip in particular.

One night it was late and I decided to stay at the William Creek Hotel. I had a long breakfast with plenty of conversation next morning and they would not take money for the accommodation or breakfast. People were like that 30 or 40 years ago.

I was mindful that there had been murders in the Australian outback and Arlene always warned: 'Don't stop on the road.' On this particular trip, I had left Kingoonya and while travelling to Coober Pedy got tired and stopped to set up camp. I fired up the Primus, cooked a steak, had some billy tea and then settled down in the back of the Land Cruiser for a rest.

I kept hearing noises and thinking of what Arlene had said. There were shadows flickering and dingoes passing then 15 camels in an Afghan camel train went by. I was just settling down again when the train tracks a few metres away came alive with a locomotive blaring its horn as it raced past with its carriages.

I finally got up and drove to Coober Pedy with every door of the vehicle locked. I reached the Opal Inn, owned by the late Bob Coro, at 4.30 am – safe at last.

But despite the accolades and camaraderie involved in the job, Geoff Brock began to feel disillusioned as the company's outlook started to change. It was 1979. He had been in the role for five years. Perhaps he had wearied of the frontier challenge. His happy marriage had survived the pressures of his career and he and Arlene had become the proud parents of daughter Hayley.

Geoff had his eye on a roadhouse in Port Augusta, the BP

Transcontinental. In partnership with a Marree identity, he took on the roadhouse, running it around the clock, taking on the Toyo brand with 150 tyres on display and boosting the staff from 17 to 47 in two years.

'We built up the spare tyres because we were basically the first available supplier and fitter to those travellers coming across the Nullarbor Desert,' Geoff Brock said.

> *We had a 24-hour restaurant and roadhouse. I would start work at 5.30 am and not get home until 10 or 11 at night. We bought our ice from a local supplier and then acquired an ice-making machine, which we operated overnight. We were packing about 100 bags a night.*
>
> *The other aspects of the business were going well. At one weekend, we did grease-ups and lubes and sold $2000 worth of tyres – what would that be worth today?*

Arlene provided the support at home that Geoff Brock so desperately needed, cared for baby Hayley, and occasionally saw friends who came around for coffee mornings.

'She didn't drive at that time,' he said.

With the business thriving and money flowing into the bank, it was a shock when the roadhouse partnership with the Marree identity collapsed. After two-and-a-half years of hard work at the roadhouse, the couple was forced to leave Port Augusta, suffering financial losses.

Perhaps ready to take on forces seemingly bigger than himself, Geoff Brock moved back to Port Pirie ready to take the first steps in his political career. But first he and Arlene needed a home. They inspected a house in Esmond Road Extension in Port Pirie and were confronted by purple walls and linoleum turning up at the corners.

'It certainly didn't impress me, but Norm Tully was the real estate salesman and he spruiked it as having a lot of potential,' Geoff said. 'My mother-in-law said she could feel a vibe, that the house had so much love in it. We bought it for $10,000.'

Adding an extension and doing a lot of renovating, the couple stayed for 12 years and were much loved by some 'fantastic' neighbours. Although the folks were friendly, the area had shocking roads. When it rained about 30 families were unable to get into their properties because of the mud and slush. Nearby Leonard Avenue had weeds in the middle of the road.

The problem was exacerbated because the area fell within the Pirie District Council, a country-style municipality surrounding the bigger Port Pirie City Council. It became complicated when the state government annexed the area to the city council.

Seizing the opportunity, Geoff approached the city council to demand street improvements. He was told the new area had been part of the city council for only five months and they would have to wait at least 20 years for any works to be done. This was despite the council overseer becoming bogged in his car while inspecting the area and needing a tractor to pull him out.

Furious residents took the issue to then mayor, the late Bill Jones, who arranged for them to speak to councillors at a meeting. Geoff Brock and fellow resident Tony Connole were sitting in the council chambers when, five minutes before they were due to speak, about 85 ratepayers turned up and stood with them in a show of strength.

'We had a good hearing. The residents later enjoyed a

community barbecue to celebrate at Moresby Park, a venue we had built,' Geoff recalled.

> *In those days I didn't know what councils actually did other than look after roads. We had a few drinks at the barbecue and when I woke next morning I was reminded that I had been nominated to represent the residents in Spencer Ward of the city council at the next elections.*

In a taste of what was to come in future elections, Geoff Brock won his seat in a landslide. He amassed more votes than the other five candidates' combined tally. Within 12 months of joining the council, Geoff had ensured that the roads were improved, thanks to state and federal grants.

His record for getting things done became so well known that one resident approached him demanding action on an issue because he had 'voted' for him. Geoff got the work done, but was quietly amused that the resident, in fact, lived in Solomontown Ward represented by Cr Frank 'Hollywood' Mezzino. He knew this because he frequently studied the electoral roll and knew who lived where.

When the Brocks had returned to Port Pirie, Geoff had applied successfully for a position as an orderly at the hospital. But in a turn of events that shaped his destiny, he was told by hospital superintendent Arthur Dawson that he would not be hired 'because you can do better'.

Although crestfallen Geoff found his career was about to benefit from the actions of his father-in-law Jack Cabrie, an electrician at the smelters, who put in a good word for him at the plant. Then followed an aptitude test for a clerical role. Geoff flunked. Undaunted, he applied for a labourer's job in the day gang led by the late 'Paddles' Young.

'My very first job at the smelters was on the jack-hammer,' Geoff said.

He and other workers found themselves on the lead floor breaking up previously molten metal that had solidified after overflowing the gutter. It was half-an-inch deep in places; in others six. Geoff chose to remove the bullion in the shallowest spot only to be told to move to a thicker area, but the blade of the jackhammer became stuck in the lead. They had to wait for a lead-burner with oxygen equipment to free the blade.

'So we sat there for four hours. I couldn't believe it,' Geoff said.

The jokes ran thick and fast at the smelter, sometimes at the expense of the less experienced workers. Geoff was once working on the blast furnace in searing temperatures with a big shovel to separate molten slag and lead. There was a problem involving a ladle, as big as a wardrobe, which had to be pulled forwards by a forklift.

With molten slag spilling from the ladle, Geoff, who had never driven a forklift, was asked to tackle the manoeuvre. The ladle jerked with every move of his foot on the throttle and he was relieved of the task after only about two minutes in the role. One of his colleagues later suggested he claim forklift allowance in his pay for his short-lived duties. Upon speaking to a superior, he was unceremoniously told that no such thing existed and he had better forget the idea.

'I was surprised I lasted at the smelters for 30 years,' Geoff laughed.

His next job there was as an engineering clerk with responsibility for many young apprentices. Wandering the stacks of lead ingots on the wharf, he was also in control of shipping of the product by sea, rail and road. He saw the transition in haulage from luffing cranes to gantry cranes.

The luffing cranes could unload 50 tonnes of metal an hour with six machines and a crew of 13 workers. This was upstaged by the gantry crane that had been floated in from Tasmania and could handle 800 tonnes an hour with a crew of two people. Geoff Brock gained his forklift and gantry crane licences and remained with this division until it was contracted to Toll Logistics.

'I didn't go with the new contractor. I elected to stay with the company,' he said.

He then stepped into the multi-million-dollar world of contracts for the smelters, handling agreements and terms with 15 firms. He was also responsible for the change-houses, weighing scales, roadwork and masonry. By this time, he was in the midst of serving six years as a councillor for Spencer Ward amid speculation in the community that he could go further in local politics.

When Geoff Brock worked in the smelter at Port Pirie, few at work had an inkling that he would one day hold high office. The now-retired Barry Wilton was the manager of engineering and maintenance with responsibility for logistics including shipping and transport where Geoff worked in the late 1980s and early 1990s.

'I didn't closely supervise him because he was a couple of managerial levels removed from me,' Mr Wilton said. 'From what I can recall, he was always a friendly, popular sort of guy. His role was mostly clerical. Not many of us would have had those expectations of Mr Brock back in those days. He was a fairly quiet guy.'

Vic Hilliard, now a business adviser with the federal Industry, Innovation and Science Department, recalls a 12-month period when Geoff worked for him at the smelter: 'He hasn't got a bad bone in his body.'

Geoff recalled:

People kept saying they wanted me to run for mayor. I was not interested, but I got so much pressure from people to consider it. I was called 'gutless' so I put my name down about 10 seconds before midday when the nominations closed. There were three of us contesting for mayor: Ken Madigan, sitting mayor Denis Crisp and myself. Ken, after the distribution of preferences, won the election by about 100 votes; I was in second place.

As a result of the election rules, I had to sit out the next three years before I could rejoin local government. I became involved in the Main Street Committee with Dianne Patterson, Margie Arnold and Dianne Robertson-Smith who was the co-ordinator. Some beautiful palm trees were planted in the median strip in Ellen Street, Port Pirie, as a result of the committee's work.

Under Ken Madigan's leadership in the 1990s, the city council merged with the Pirie District Council and then again with the Crystal Brook–Redhill District Council. At one stage, the council consisted of an unwieldy 25 members, making for complicated debates and providing some challenging moments for the mayor.

Waiting in the wings was Geoff Brock who 'just wanted to represent the community without any intention of being mayor'. But he came to modify his stance, possibly with an inkling of things to come.

'If someone gives you a challenge, you have to give it a go,' he said.

Chapter 5

'I Kissed Her Goodbye'

The excitement of Geoff Brock's first foray into the mayoral race in Port Pirie was overshadowed by tragedy. He was forced to explore a new future, one vastly different from that imagined by himself and his wife Arlene.

The Brocks' life was shattered when Arlene died in a road smash near Port Pirie in 1992, 14 days before Christmas Day. Still recovering from the shock, Geoff threw himself into community work with even greater determination. His attitude to life – don't give up when you are knocked down – shines through as he speaks lovingly of his late wife and how he struggled to comprehend the loss. He held hands with Arlene one last time, as her body lay still beneath a cloth, at the funeral parlour.

'Even today, if I hear an ambulance siren, horrible feelings go through me . . . it is the same with our daughters,' he said.

The head-on crash that claimed Arlene's life happened on Port Broughton Road while she was searching for a turn-off to Warnertown. She had planned to pick up a friend then travel to Adelaide where she would be a model for a hairdresser acquaintance. This was a day off from her routine of taking her daughters Hayley and Marisa to ballet school and helping with fundraising for this dance group, reading with struggling students at school and supporting Geoff in his activities.

'In the morning, I had breakfast in the kitchen and Arlene came out and joined me,' Geoff said.

I kissed her goodbye and left for work about 6.30 am and at 8.30 am the world was destroyed, in just two hours.

After I left home for work, Arlene had dropped Marisa at Mum's place in Sixth Street and then took Hayley to Port Pirie Technical High School, on Senate Road. To pick up her friend on the way to Adelaide, she drove along Abattoirs Road on the outskirts of Port Pirie and reached the railway crossing at Warnertown. Unable to get across the track because the line was closed due to a world-record attempt by workers who were laying sleepers, she took an alternative route, but missed a turn-off. She stopped in Port Broughton Road for guidance from some Telstra workers who directed her to another turn-off, but she never made it.

There was a bend on the road.

He recited the number of the residential property on the corner, his voice wavering.

'Arlene was killed instantly and the four occupants of the other car, who had just finished night shift at the smelters where I worked, were hurt but survived,' Geoff recalled.

The ambulance, firefighters and all the major services went to the scene. Soon after, the police came to the gate of the smelters and a two-way radio call was conveyed to me from the shipping office that there was someone waiting to see me at the security gate. I thought it was a representative of the Smelters Picnic Committee seeking my signature on a cheque because I was an authorised signatory. I didn't immediately go out. When I reached the gates, I saw a police officer standing there. He asked whether I was Geoff Brock.

I replied, 'Yes,' and he said, 'Your wife is dead.' That is exactly what he said. I said, 'Are you joking?' and he identified our red Commodore as having been in the crash. I immediately reacted by hitting the copper. I swung and knocked him over. I then went to tell my father-in-law Jack Cabrie of the news about his daughter.

Jack worked in the electrical shop at the smelters and I blurted it out to him. He had lost his wife with cancer only 18 months before and now his only daughter had been killed. I went back to the office. I had my two-way radio on my hip and took it off and threw it into the wall. By this stage, the others knew . . . everyone knew before me.

It was just unreal.

Next came the confronting and difficult task of telling his parents and his children about the tragedy. The tension continued when he was asked at the funeral parlour to identify his late wife. At first, Geoff and his father-in-law refused to do so, even though they knew it was a legal requirement.

He eventually agreed to perform the sad duty and saw that 'Arlene didn't have a mark on her that I could see'.

'I wanted to get out. The funeral director suggested I spend some time with her or I may regret it later,' he said.

I spent an hour there, just talking to her and holding her hand. Her death changed the direction of my life and shattered our dreams into a million pieces. Not only did it affect us personally and emotionally, but it changed the whole direction of our lives. We were just moving along. I loved being a councillor and doing community work.

We had dreams of getting to an old age, sitting on the porch together, enjoying our retirement and watching our children and grandchildren grow up.

I knew I had a loving family and wife and that I was allowed to do a lot of things that were rewarding to myself and family, but were also helping the community. I was on the primary school and high school governing councils and the Smelters Picnic Committee. I reckon at one stage I was on 25 committees or organisations.

Arlene was involved in the ballet school, which the kids attended, and helped with the fundraising for the school. She also took the girls to netball. Two or three times a week, she would attend the school with the Learning Assistance Program to read to a student or in small groups to children who required that extra attention.

I worked every bit of overtime I could at the smelters to provide better opportunities for the family. Whenever we had a function, everything was ready, thanks to Arlene. My clothes would always be ready and they complemented whatever Arlene chose to wear to the event.

Our family circle was very close.

The funeral service was conducted by Pastor Ern Heyne, who had married the couple in the same Lutheran Church in Port Pirie and baptised their girls. There were 500 to 600 people there, the church was overflowing. The tributes were unbelievable.

'Kevin Victory and Graham Koch, who were car dealers at the time, provided us with a van in which to travel to the crematorium in Adelaide because our car had to be written off after the crash,' Geoff Brock said.

> *The van was available free for as long as we needed it. I could not thank Kevin and Graham enough for enabling us to have transport to attend the funeral and cremation service in Adelaide. They were just unbelievable.*
>
> *There was a flood of people coming to our house, some from Melbourne and Adelaide, as well as councillors and council workers. It was 14 days before Christmas and Arlene and I had already picked out the presents for the girls. They included tickets to the Scottish band Bay City Rollers, who were performing in Adelaide.*
>
> *I took annual leave and rostered days off to cope with the grief, but once these were exhausted, I was not ready to return to work. I spoke to the human resources department at what was then Pasminco and they said to take leave for as long as I needed.*
>
> *I took another two months off. Later, I discovered they had given me that extra time free. The company was magnificent.*

Geoff Brock brushed away tears as he recalled his wife's death and the circumstances surrounding her funeral. But he managed a smile as the conversation turned to his recent visit to students in Clare in his role as Cabinet minister with the state government. The children wanted to show him their cubby house made from a cloth draped over a dining-room table. He clambered about on the floor on his hands and knees and spoke to the youngsters about the election of their captains and co-captains.

'I said that if they were not successful in their election, they should support whoever wins,' he said. 'I said their dreams are "up there" and if someone kicks out the foundations, don't give up. These challenges and obstacles come along in your life, but you need to just move on.'

Chapter 6

Waiting Game

The seconds ticked away on New Year's Day, 1994. In downtown Port Broughton, a seaside resort near Port Pirie, Geoff Brock sat in his darkened car at 1 am contemplating his future. The seconds lengthened into minutes as he wondered whether he had been rebuffed by his newfound friend, Lyn Akker.

After the tragedy of his wife's death in 1992, Geoff was finding his feet and had asked the attractive, dark-haired Lyn on a date on New Year's Eve. They dined at a restaurant in Port Pirie then drove to Fisherman Bay, near Port Broughton, to visit Lyn's sister Debbie and her husband Bruce McDonald. As they headed back to Port Broughton from Fisherman Bay, and the clock ticked into the new year, Lyn mentioned that she needed to visit a toilet so they drove to the amenities block on the foreshore of the town.

Lyn went inside and Geoff waited . . . and waited . . . and waited.

Not being the most confident of suitors, he wondered whether she had gone out the back window and jilted him. Finally, she emerged, pale and weak, having suffered food poisoning from the restaurant meal. In a gallant gesture, he put his jacket around the shivering Lyn and they returned to Port Pirie.

As they farewelled each other, he commented it had been a great night – despite the after-dinner diversion – and asked whether he could see her again. She replied, 'I suppose – when?' to which he responded enthusiastically, 'This afternoon?'

So began a relationship in which the couple spent many hours talking about their respective children and families. With their daughters and sons, they became a blended family, one which has endured and flourished for 22 years, inspiring Geoff Brock on his journey through work and politics.

Lyn's sincerity has been a hallmark of their life together. 'She speaks her mind and is very family orientated. She did a good job raising her kids after her divorce,' Geoff said. 'Other than being most attractive, she is one of those people you can sit and talk to. My family always came first. With my wife Arlene gone, I dedicated myself to the girls.'

Ironically, like the late Arlene, Lynn is a hairdresser and she kept the Brock daughters' hair immaculate. The girls had appointments at Lyn's salon in Ellen Street, as did Geoff amid his busy schedule as a councillor, smelter worker and community volunteer.

'That is how our conversation started – discussing affairs in general while Lyn cut my hair,' he said. Things were also changing on the home front.

'When my daughters were ready to move on in their lives, they decided it was time we looked at getting another house because of all the memories that remained there,' he said

I had been in a relationship with another lady, Sue. She was my saviour in that interim period. I could talk with her and fill that vacuum in my life; confide in someone outside my family. But when our relationship ended, my daughters said I should ask Lyn on a date.

I remember one night I had had a few drinks and caught a taxi home to find the girls sitting on the front veranda. They

started encouraging me to see Lyn. So I later found some hair curlers Lyn had left in the girls' room and went to the salon on the pretext of returning them – and planning to ask her out.

I am pretty shy around women and the invitation didn't happen. Later, we had a conversation about the possibility of my moving house and Lyn replied that maybe the venture needed a 'woman's touch'.

I asked whether she was available to have a look. Lyn accompanied me to one of the houses for inspection where we met real-estate agent Alan Craigie, who had an office next to Lyn's salon.

He said, 'What's going on here?'

'Nothing,' we both said, another opportunity missed, but the girls encouraged me to keep trying.

Lyn refused an invitation from Geoff to the council's Christmas party, but finally agreed to dinner on New Year's Eve and romance ensued.

Just as their lives and interests merged, Geoff Brock was involved in the amalgamation of the Risdon and Proprietary Football clubs in a move that affected Lyn's twin sons Ady and Nicky Akker. Both young men played for Proprietary in 1993 when Geoff was appointed independent chairman to oversee the amalgamation. He was not a member of either club and had played only a few matches for Port Football Club. Lynn also had a connection to Proprietary through her brother-in-law and star wingman Bruce McDonald. Bruce and his wife, Debbie, Lyn's sister, lived in a beautiful, rambling house on Senate Road in Port Pirie.

One night the McDonalds mentioned that they were looking at

moving to a property in the country at Bungama on the outskirts of Port Pirie. Lyn and Geoff both burst out with the request: 'If you are going to sell your house, give us first option.'

As the eventual successful buyers, they made further improvements to the house. Geoff puts up Christmas light decorations every year and can be seen crouching in the garden, pulling up weeds and planting shrubs. Often in the middle of mowing the lawn, he is called over by a passer-by to discuss an issue of the moment.

After facing personal and professional challenges, the couple settled in for the long haul together. 'I always wanted to be married again, but Lyn wanted to wait and let the families adjust to this financial and emotional commitment that we had made,' Geoff said. 'I asked her to marry me and she said we should wait until the kids are grown up and here I am 22 years later.

'We have not married, but we are committed to each other. You never know what might happen.'

With a more settled life, Geoff breezed into the mayoralty of Port Pirie in 2003 and then was re-elected in 2006. This was followed by a decision – in defiance of Lyn's wishes – to quit the smelter so that he could speak freely on the lead pollution issue. His resignation was a $100,000 financial hit to the family, but it allowed him to be free of conflict-of-interest rules in the *Local Government Act* that blocked him from defending his employer, then known as Pasminco. The company had been generous in allowing him to pursue his local government interests, although he was working up to 50 hours a week at the smelter and up to 50 hours a week on council business.

After his resignation, he received a $50,000 yearly mayoral allowance. But the decision sparked a series of events that ultimately led to his balance-of-power deliberations after the 2014 state election and his role in the rescue of Nyrstar, the current owner of the smelter.

'Everything lined up. If I had stayed at the smelter, would it have happened?' Geoff Brock said.

> *Lyn was not happy, but I felt a weight was lifted from my shoulders when I resigned and took a package. The blood-lead levels in Port Pirie's children were rising at the time. I had been unable to defend what the smelter was doing to alleviate the problem. We were being lampooned nationally about high blood-lead levels among our children, even though there were vast improvements at the smelter after it came out of administration in 2004.*
>
> *I had been unable to comment about blood-lead results because I worked for the company and it was a conflict under the Local Government Act. The company was looking at enclosing the blast furnace to reduce emissions. I was mayor and they had just come out of administration. If I started mentioning Pasminco or Zinifex, as it was called afterwards, it could be seen to be an attempt to improve my job security.*
>
> *Lead was still a big issue and, after my resignation, I was able to be more involved with the Ten by Ten committee and talk with the state government together with the council chief executive officer at the time, Ian Burfitt. I could defend the smelter, if needed, and comment on future directions.*
>
> *The unions were fantastic during the administration process.*

One of the key figures in negotiations for the future of the plant was Bill Shorten, then president of the Australian Workers Union and later federal Labor leader. Mr Shorten actually visited the site to discuss options for the survival of the business.

'The unions and senior management worked on a proposal for the administrators that showcased what could be done when a big company gets into trouble,' Geoff Brock said. 'The bank, instead of foreclosing, took equity in the company and then we traded out of administration.'

Like the smelter, the Port Pirie council had also been experiencing an upheaval. After mergers in the 1990s of the city council with neighbouring councils, the civic benches had an almost unmanageable 25 elected members. The meetings were chaired by Mayor Ken Madigan, who is praised by Geoff for his statesman-like qualities and for his role as chairman of the economy-boosting regional development board. Critics of this era in Port Pirie's history point to the many projects that were floated as possible economic saviours, but which never eventuated. Those who defend the situation, say that it was a case of nothing ventured, nothing gained – these options had to be explored.

'We had been promised so many things: the container plant, the brass factory, the magnesium plant,' Geoff Brock said.

At the time of the 2006 mayoral race, only the magnesium plant was still in contention.

'No other promised activity eventuated. I think people were looking for change – and that is no disrespect to Ken because he did a fantastic job,' he said.

Geoff Brock was elected mayor in 2002 in what the local newspaper, the *Recorder*, dubbed a 'Brockslide'. The late Rita Blieschke was the deputy mayor. Geoff immediately began a campaign for renewal by calling a meeting at which he planned to re-energise his elected members.

'I indicated to them we were on a journey and, if they didn't want to be aboard, then they should get off. The council was united. They wanted to get things done and were sick of things not happening,' he recalled. The elected members were really hyped up.

Soon after, the council parted company with chief executive officer John Vucic, replacing him with the high-powered local government veteran, Ian Burfitt. Mr Burfitt had strong credentials and it was an amazing feat for Port Pirie to lure him from Port Lincoln where he was in a similar role. Before that he had worked at Clare council.

'He came to Port Pirie, was successful and we started to hit the ground and get some visible results,' Geoff said.

> *There was less talk and more action. People were resisting him because he wanted change but it was happening anyway. We negotiated with then Premier Mike Rann and brought him to Port Pirie to discuss the old foreshore area including the Conaust and the Marine and Harbours Board sites, which were Crown land. This land was pivotal in changing the image of the city.*
>
> *Mr Rann was talking in millions of dollars that he wanted in payment to the government for the land. He turned and said, 'What do you want me to do, give it to you for nothing?'*
>
> *I said, 'Yes, Premier,' and he did.*
>
> *Mr Burfitt and council oversaw the creation of Flinders View Park recreational area near the wharf. It was rejuvenated. The*

old oil berth was to be developed for visits by the sail-training vessel One And All and pontoons were to be installed for the Blessing of the Fleet ceremony activities.

Unfortunately, different councils have different views and that aspect of the project was never completed.

Despite the euphoria surrounding the new council, a nail was hammered into the coffin of the proposed magnesium plant by then Regional Development Minister Rory McEwen. Mr McEwen called for a review of due diligence of the project.

'I got on the radio and blasted the minister,' Geoff Brock recalled.

I questioned how he had the gall to call for a government review of a private company that wanted to invest in our city. Far away, Mr McEwen was shaving while listening to the radio and cut his face.

He rang council chief executive officer Ian Burfitt and criticised my comments. He asked how this 'upstart' could dare question his intentions. Mr Burfitt defended me. It was one of my first brushes with the state government.

Geoff Brock's working relationship with Ian Burfitt was so good that they were nicknamed 'B1 and B2', in reference to the *Bananas in Pyjamas* ABC TV show. Ian Burfitt impressed the council by immediately buying a house in Port Pirie after he signed his contract to join the team. He then scrapped plans to spend a week unpacking so that he could troubleshoot a problem with the grass surface of the council-owned Memorial Oval.

Another project tackled by Mr Burfitt with gusto was the improvement to landscaped areas beside Three Chain Road.

'We knew where we stood with him,' Geoff said.

Every weeknight, 'B1 and B2' would travel the streets of the region by car for up to 90 minutes. The chief executive officer would show the mayor what projects had been achieved earlier in the day. 'We got lots of things done,' Geoff Brock said.

Achievements included relocating the council depot, creating the foreshore park, planning a new library, undergrounding power lines in Solomontown and finalising the proposal for burial of the power lines in Florence Street, and a million-dollar revamp of the swimming pool.

Perhaps relishing his free hand, Ian Burfitt suggested ripping up the then-dilapidated Solomontown Beach jetty and replacing it with pontoons. Geoff Brock locked horns with his mate to resist the proposal and the jetty was upgraded instead.

'There would have been an outcry from the community if we demolished the jetty,' he said.

Port Pirie has a wide range of people and most are down-to-earth. We need to listen to them. We are the first provincial city in South Australia and there is a great sense of community here.

When a crisis arises, people are keen to support people in need, whether it be financially or emotionally. When the smelter was owned by Pasminco and was in crisis, the town was looking at building a helipad at the hospital. People dug deep to raise more than $100,000 for the project when our major industry faced an uncertain future.

> *No matter what you do or where you come from, our residents treat each other the same. We all come into this world the same way and do different things in our lives, but we will go out the same way. We have had some tragedies, but we support each other.*

Geoff Brock's obvious respect for his community was reflected in 2006 when he was re-elected unopposed as mayor. Residents sensed he might be capable of more. While speaking to the Rotary Club of Port Pirie, he was approached by guests suggesting that he run for state politics. Soon after, over a cup of coffee at Caffe Florence, he confided to me, then managing editor of the *Recorder*, that he was thinking of running for the seat of Frome at a by-election in 2009.

It was the first time Geoff had shared his plans. I asked which political party he would represent. He replied, 'None,' he would be an Independent candidate.

In subsequent weeks, he had overtures from both major political parties offering to endorse his run for office. Having been rebuffed by Geoff Brock, the then Opposition leader Martin Hamilton-Smith rode his motorcycle to Port Pirie, with prospective Frome candidate Terry Boylan on the back, to promote the Liberals.

'We had a discussion in my office,' Geoff said.

> *In a telephone call, I was also quizzed by a Labor identity from Port Augusta. The then deputy mayor, Neville Wilson, called at my office to say he would run for the National Party in Frome. I could not let Neville know of my intentions as they had not yet been made public, other than confidentially to the managing editor of the* Recorder.

I was going to run as an Independent despite the calls from people in the Liberal and Labor parties. I never seriously considered accepting anything from either party.

Frankly, I never expected to win.

Chapter 7

Keystone Kops

The battle for the seat of Frome, based around Port Pirie, was a David versus Goliath encounter in 2009. Geoff Brock's campaign committee of five people would take on the political machines of the two major parties in a 'Keystone Kops' caper. In a comedy of errors, his rivals lodged complaints under the *Electoral Act* about his posters and banners, and claimed the most strategic spots to display their electioneering material. At the polling booths, his team handing out how-to-vote cards was outnumbered. Humbled, but determined, the group took stock of their chance of success.

They did not expect to win the seat being contested by the Liberals, Labor and other minor parties. Both major parties had been rebuffed in their early overtures to enlist Geoff to represent them in the race for votes. He said their approaches somehow worked in the opposite way to that intended by making him feel even more confident that he was on the right track as an independent candidate.

'If you want to do something, then have a go at it,' he said.

The by-election in Frome was called to fill a vacancy created by the surprise retirement of ex-premier Rob Kerin, of Crystal Brook. Mr Kerin had held the seat comfortably since it was formed 15 years earlier. Observers were mystified about why he chose to force a by-election rather than wait until the scheduled state election in 2010.

The by-election was called in early December 2008 with the poll due on 17 January 2009. Both parties brought forward their 2010 preselected candidates, Liberal Terry Boylan, a local policeman, and for Labor John Rohde, a postal worker and community radio announcer.

A couple of weeks after nominations had opened, Geoff Brock lodged his paperwork.

> *Once I had lodged my nomination, my candidacy became public and I began visiting areas outside Port Pirie to campaign because these were also important in terms of potential voting support. As mayor, I had an understanding of country areas such as Redhill and Koolunga. I was retired at that time and needed to do some campaigning in Clare, a Liberal stronghold.*
>
> *Quite often I would get a call from a Port Pirie resident with a local government issue and I would always attend to that rather than go out on the campaign trail. They would ask me about my electioneering and I would say, 'You come first.'*
>
> *On one occasion I went to Clare to talk to people in the street, but most turned out to be tourists who didn't know anything about the election. It was the festive season and wineries were having their vintage harvest. People were away with their families on holiday. I would have visited Clare for no more than one-and-a-half days while attempting to run the campaign there and won only 30 votes in the poll. I didn't know anyone there.*

In Port Pirie, he avoided doorknocking and went about his electioneering in the same style that he had used as a councillor and mayoral candidate. He walked the streets, stopping to have a chat with shoppers. He avoided challenging people to vote for him.

Geoff Brock's campaign had a boost when high-profile state upper house Independent MP Nick Xenophon responded to his plea for help. The charismatic, like-minded Mr Xenophon appeared at Pirie Plaza Shopping Centre to endorse his friend after driving up from Adelaide. The visit came during pre-poll voting, a crucial time for the campaign.

'Everyone knew Nick and most people knew who I was in my role as mayor,' Geoff said. 'His visit and words of encouragement gave me a boost and a bit more belief in myself.'

On show in the shopping mall during their visit was a billboard, which Geoff Brock had not sought permission to display. Luckily, there was no backlash from authorities, unlike events surrounding promotional material later in the campaign.

With five weeks remaining until poll day, Geoff drew together his committee of five to work for his election. His first pick was brother-in-law Graham Nichols, Geoff's sister Mary's husband. He stepped in as campaign director with 'zero' experience. The other committee members were former Telecom technicians Peter Baur and the late Andy Hern, Italian community president Cr Dino Gadaleta, and monumental mason Sav Degiglio.

'The only one with some experience in campaigns was me – and that was bugger all,' Geoff Brock said.

> *We had no bloody idea. It was the blind leading the blind. We would have meetings and start with great intentions, but just struggled along. We had a few red wines and beers – we were going to change the world.*

I spent just under $10 000 on my campaign. It was a shoestring budget. It was a 'budget' budget. I pulled money out of my super fund to pay for it. We had no thoughts of winning. We had the excitement, great vibes. It was an experience and we just enjoyed it and had a lot of fun. I didn't have the financial or physical resources to match the major political machines so we went along and experienced the adventure of our lives.

Few of the committee members had been involved in politics. Some had never even voted in a council election. But Geoff Brock had a growing sense of destiny about the group and he thanks them for their support to this day.

'They didn't ask for favours,' he said, 'or financial assistance, even though I offered to cover some of their expenses when they worked to put up my signs. They did it because they wanted to do it, which is rare these days.'

Trouble hit the team when a complaint was lodged about the size of their pink-hued banners displayed around the electorate. Such complaints are made anonymously under the *Electoral Act*. The banners were supposed to be no bigger than a square metre so Mr Brock's had to be taken down, stapled and folded to comply with regulations, and put up again.

There were also problems with the corflute signs that adorned Stobie poles. They were the right size, but lacked holes through which to draw twine to fasten them to the poles. The first ones had makeshift holes punched into them, but they ripped apart and fell to the ground. Geoff paid for 250 signs to be fitted with metal eyelets so they could be displayed properly.

During pre-polling voting at the old courthouse, in Florence Street, Port Pirie, a canvas banner was deemed over-size.

'I could not get more of them made up because I couldn't afford it,' Geoff recalled.

The volunteers distributing his how-to-vote cards were outnumbered at the old courthouse by those representing the other contenders. But the old-fashioned sense of community shone through, just as it had on the fateful night a couple of months earlier when Geoff Brock, speaking at a Rotary event, had been approached and asked to run for the seat just vacated by Rob Kerin. Others, impressed with his performance as mayor, had also challenged him to run for office.

He had discussed his options with partner Lyn Akker. Defying her prediction that he had no hope of success, he kept mulling on the idea. He was emboldened because the retiring member had been unable to devote all his time to the electorate because of his duties as premier in 2001 and 2002. Geoff felt the timing was right for a change of representation in the House of Assembly for the seat of Frome.

'I have a bit of pride and didn't want to be labelled gutless for not running,' he said.

But Geoff still suffered twinges of doubt, particularly when his campaign launch a fortnight before the poll attracted only 30 people to the BH Community Club, a one-time bastion of the working man. On returning home, he saw a Liberal Party campaign car, festooned with flags and banners and illuminated signs, parked outside his home. Before he could investigate, the phone rang inside the house. On the line was a national newspaper reporter wanting to interview him about his prospects. He was in mid-sentence when he heard the front gate to his property being opened and saw a Liberal campaigner approaching the house.

'I told the journalist I would call her back,' he recalled.

The campaigner blurted out the words, 'Good afternoon, sir,' before realising he was trying to persuade the Independent candidate to vote against himself.

The irony did not end there. Soon after the campaigners targeted Pirie West and knocked on the door of one of Geoff Brock's daughters, Hayley. She quickly set the record straight by saying her father was Geoff Brock and he could count on her vote.

Technicalities continued to plague the campaign. On the Thursday before poll day, he was notified that the corflute signs on Stobie poles around the electorate breached regulations because they lacked authorisation and printing information. They would have to be torn down.

Members of the campaign committee discussed the problem and came up with a novel solution: they would cut the bottoms off how-to-vote cards and sticky-tape them onto the bottom of the signs. The desired information would be displayed. All they had to do was travel around to 250 signs that night to fix the situation. This meant covering up to 100 kilometres.

'I didn't have time to take them all down and have them reprinted. It was also a matter of extra cost,' Geoff Brock said. He still has a thousand of the original how-to-vote cards from that first poll foray. Today he and Lyn use them for notepads at home or for scribbling a shopping list.

Supermarket visits were a minor concern as the poll day approached. On the Friday night before the by-election, Geoff took Lyn to dinner at the Sportsman Tavern in Solomontown to show his appreciation for her support during the campaign. As they opened the hotel door to enter the dining room, they were confronted by Liberal leader Martin Hamilton-Smith, members of the shadow Cabinet, and the Liberals' Frome candidate Terry Boylan enjoying a meal.

'I went up and said, "Welcome to Port Pirie, guys." As Lyn and I were leaving after our meal we overheard one of them say, "That's the last we will see of him."'

Next day was voting day and once again the Brock crew was caught short. There were only seven helpers to hand out how-to-vote cards at the polling booths. Geoff could not join the volunteers because candidates were banned from being within a certain distance of booths, except when casting their vote. Every television station sent reporters to cover Mr Brock casting his ballot at the Baptist Church in Hannan Street.

'When I put my ballot in the box, the cameras were flashing,' Geoff said.

> *I didn't talk to people before I went in. I had to say that I couldn't speak to them until after they had voted. As we came out, people would give me a 'high five' – or not. I took drinks to the helpers, but made sure I stayed away from the booths, not wanting any more trouble with the electoral returning officer.*
>
> *We had promotional material at 20 of the booths. By the time we went to put banners on fences, both major parties had picked the best spots to display theirs. The big parties have the most resources. They were concentrating on Frome, not looking at other electorates, because there was only the one by-election in the state that day.*

Geoff explained his decision to run as an Independent. 'I had decided that if I were ever going to run for office, it would not be for one of the major parties,' he said.

> *I had approaches, both directly and indirectly, from three parties. I was thinking, Why are they interested? They already had their 2010 candidates lined up and they could contest the by-election. Being supported by a party would have helped financially, but I could not make myself publicly answerable to any political party.*

As the hours ticked by on poll day, Geoff Brock felt he had nothing to lose and everything to gain. Or did he?

Chapter 8

A Streetcar Named Desire

The gleaming, multi-coloured tram turned from King William Street into North Terrace in the heart of Adelaide and stopped. It was just a short stroll from the ornate corridors and stone facade of a building that dominates South Australian life – Parliament House.

Outside the building was the state's newest parliamentarian, Geoff Brock. Only five days after being declared in a by-election as the Member for Frome, Geoff had been summoned to the House of Assembly for his first day in the job. It had been a bumpy few hours with the new MP receiving little or no guidance from experienced politicians in the major parties. This was understandable – he was an Independent with allegiance to no one and goodwill from few.

Geoff was heading from his makeshift office to the tram and then to an apartment at Glenelg where he was to spend the night. The tram door slid open and Mr Brock climbed in, clutching his parliamentarian's badge and mindful that as an MP he was entitled to free public transport. He produced his badge to the conductor who seemed perplexed.

'I am the new Member for Frome,' Geoff Brock explained. The conductor thought a moment, then said, 'Ahhh, the Game of Frome?' obviously confusing Geoff's title with the television series *Game of Thrones*.

Geoff Brock had gone from being featured on national and state news programs to being just another unknown passenger among thousands on the public transport network. It highlighted the long road that lay ahead and Geoff, the shy man from the bush, was under no illusions about his newfound role.

That night, as he lay his head on the pillow in his hotel room, Geoff's mind raced with thoughts of what he could achieve in office. His momentary humiliation on the tram contrasted with several days of fame and elation during the election count when he dramatically rose from being almost 3000 votes behind to clinch the seat of Frome on preferences and take the oath of office.

He had spent close to $10,000 on his campaign, with no outside donations apart from $200 raised at a dinner hosted by supporter Cr Dino Gadaleta at the Italian councillor's home in Port Pirie. 'I didn't ask anyone for financial assistance because I had decided to run as an Independent.'

After casting his vote on election day, he had returned home to waiting television cameras. He invited exhausted media representatives to join him at the celebratory barbecue, but they were too busy reporting on his campaign for office and possible political fallout. Several of his supporters, including Peter Baur, were sitting in the shade of the hedge monitoring the poll on their laptops.

'At the end of the night, I was almost 3000 votes behind the Liberal candidate Terry Boylan,' Geoff Brock said. 'I did not think in my wildest dreams that I could win because I was so far behind.'

A couple of days later, while counting of ballots continued, Geoff Brock travelled to the Australian Open tennis tournament in Melbourne to represent the Port Pirie Regional Council as mayor. He had been invited by Tennis Australia because Port Pirie was hosting an international tennis tournament of its own that year.

After flying back to Adelaide, Geoff's mobile phone came alive with calls and messages.

One message was from the *Advertiser* and, according to Geoff Brock, it asked whether he was conceding defeat. When he asked the media outlet about his polling, he was told he was in third spot, a long way behind.

'What about preferences?' he replied.

The newspaper told him the two-party preferred vote was about 56 per cent to 44 per cent, well and truly in favour of the Liberals.

Geoff Brock felt uneasy, but conceded defeat and offered his congratulations through the newspaper to Mr Boylan. His next call came from Frome returning officer Nick Borlase who said absentee, postal and pre-poll votes could be counted on the Saturday after the election. Mr Borlase said this would be followed by the declaration of the poll taking place earlier than previously scheduled on the following Thursday because of administrative reasons.

'Again, I questioned whether he had counted all the preference votes before the absentee, postal and pre-poll votes,' Geoff Brock said.

> *He replied that he had not and would count the absentee, postal and pre-poll votes first then count all the votes for preferences. He told me that I could get some of the 20,000 votes still to be counted, not just absentee, postal and pre-poll votes, unlike the information I had received from the* Advertiser *journalist.*
>
> *I rang the newspaper and was told my earlier comments about conceding defeat had just gone up on the AdelaideNow website. I said they would have to take it off the website because*

I was not conceding, owing to the preference votes still to be counted.

Next thing, Liberal leader Martin Hamilton-Smith's staff member, Craig, rang and said, 'I want to congratulate you.' When I asked what this was about he explained he wanted to congratulate me for conceding defeat. I replied that I was not conceding and I owed it to the people who supported me to stay until the last kick.

Craig's response: 'You may as well go with dignity . . . you have no chance in hell of winning this election.'

Geoff Brock was up against the might of the Liberal Party machine.

Several hours later, upon returning home, he picked up the local newspaper the *Recorder* to read a front-page report: Mr Hamilton-Smith had claimed victory for his candidate. Mr Boylan and his wife Denise were pictured celebrating their triumph.

'I wondered what was going on here because we still had the declaration votes to count on Saturday,' Geoff Brock said.

With the primary votes counted, he was in third spot behind John Rohde; Terry Boylan led the poll. As preferences were distributed, Geoff Brock was elevated to second spot by 30 votes. The support was from a variety of sources including the Greens, One Nation – and the Nationals' Neville Wilson, a fellow civic leader on the Port Pirie council. Cr Wilson's preferences were widely credited with putting Geoff into second spot, but Geoff says that is a myth.

'It was a mixture of support, including many preferences from the Greens,' he said.

As a result of Geoff Brock's move to second and John Rohde's being relegated to third, Mr Rohde was eliminated from the count and his preferences distributed. As expected, these strongly favoured Mr Brock who kept hammering away on a solar-powered pocket calculator to assess his chances.

'I rang John Rohde to commiserate on his failed third attempt at state politics and began the frustrating wait on the Saturday while they finished counting the preferences,' he said.

> *I gave up trying to calculate the preferences on my little machine. I went back into the garden at home and waited around. It seemed like an eternity. My brother-in-law Tony Richardson was a scrutineer and he was inexperienced like the rest of us. Both major parties had more than one scrutineer. After a few hours, Tony rang to say congratulations. I had won by 665 votes. The pressure lifted. It was emotional. I couldn't believe I had won after being so far behind.*

Geoff Brock received 80 per cent of Labor's preferences to achieve his win. Returning officer Nick Borlase rejected a call from the Liberals for a recount, saying the poll was the most scrutinised election he had ever seen.

'Well done to my scrutineer Tony for working on my behalf,' Geoff Brock said.

In a 27 January front-page report headlined 'Back From The Brink', the *Recorder* highlighted how Geoff Brock had conceded defeat, but three days later was a winner. He revealed how he had snatched victory from the jaws of defeat and admitted he had mistakenly conceded defeat in an interview with the newspaper. His voice hoarse from rounds of interviews, he said he was at a loss to understand Terry Boylan's call for a recount. Defending his actions,

Terry Boylan pointed to the fact that if 16 people had voted for the Liberals in second preferences, it would have excluded Geoff Brock from the count and Geoff would have lost the election.

On the page with the election report was an editorial sounding a warning based on the fact that the previous local Independent member Ted Connelly had rejoined the Labor Party in the 1970s after being elected to office. It noted that Mr Brock, who has never been a member of a political party, had given his word against taking a similar path.

Earlier in the campaign, Geoff had denied anonymous claims that he had spoken to Attorney-General Michael Atkinson about planning an allegiance with Labor. He said his dealings with Mr Atkinson were limited to speaking to him as mayor at the Blessing of the Fleet ball in September of the previous year before he decided to become an Independent candidate for the seat.

'They are slinging mud and mud has never stuck to me. I have not made any deals with the Labor Party,' he was quoted as saying in the newspaper. He said he had been approached by both the Liberals and Labor, but was not interested in 'selling out to major political parties'.

The report said Labor candidate John Rohde had listed Geoff Brock as his second preference on his how-to-vote card. But Geoff explained that it was because Labor would not back the Liberals, Nationals or minor parties as a political strategy, leaving him as the only option. Geoff Brock gave his preferences to Nationals candidate and deputy mayor Neville Wilson and thirdly Mr Rohde.

When Geoff Brock attended the declaration of the poll, he automatically relinquished his role as the town's first citizen.

Attending the noon ceremony at the old courthouse in Port Pirie were Geoff and his partner Lyn Akker, Terry and Denise Boylan, leading Liberal Vickie Chapman and John Rohde.

With the official ceremony out of the way and parliament resuming on the following Tuesday, Geoff and Lyn then packed their bags for Adelaide for orientation at Parliament House on the Monday. Geoff strolled along North Terrace with partner Lyn and marvelled at the 'huge' Parliament House building. 'Here we are. It is really happening,' he said.

After being bombarded with information about how to conduct himself in his new role and setting up in his temporary office near the door of the House of Assembly, Geoff Brock was approached by another Independent, Kris Hanna, who had distributed how-to-vote cards for Geoff on election day. Mr Hanna took him for coffee in the Members' Lounge where he met Dr Such for the first time. He then sat on the crossbench in parliament, a lonely figure uncertain about what he was supposed to be doing. Lyn and a friend from his council days, Brenton Vanstone, were sitting in the gallery.

Fortunately, his future mentor and fellow Independent Bob Such, later to play a key role in Geoff Brock's kingmaker deliberations, was by this time sitting nearby in the House and told him there was no need to sit in the chamber all day. He explained that politicians came and went during the sitting sessions.

> *Dr Such was sitting two places up from me on the crossbench and invited me for another cup of tea. My introduction to parliament was a baptism of fire. I didn't have a political party behind me to show me the ropes but members from both sides of politics came to congratulate me after I was sworn in.*

It was the biggest learning phase of my life. I had to keep asking everyone where my office was because I was still confused. I eventually found the Blue Room in the basement where you could have lunch and dinner.

The hallways, carpet and polished wood . . . it was amazing to see all that history around me.

In the whirlwind first days of office, Geoff Brock lacked an MP's car under the leasing arrangements available to politicians. As Lyn needed their car to return to Port Pirie, Geoff was left to catch the tram.

He was introduced to the long-winded nature of parliamentary speeches on the day he was allocated a car at Thebarton's Fleet SA depot. 'I was listening to the Liberals' Vickie Chapman in the House of Assembly before I left for Thebarton,' he said. 'I travelled to the depot, did the necessary arrangements, returned in the car to the car park and then went into the House only to find that Vickie was still speaking.'

He was told it would take six months to obtain a new leased car, but if he wanted a used vehicle, he could speak to Treasurer Kevin Foley.

'I felt some apprehension at that time because Mr Foley and I had many disagreements while I was mayor,' Geoff Brock said. 'But he kindly arranged for me to get a used vehicle and I was very grateful because otherwise I would not have been able to get out into the electorate.'

Mr Brock's maiden speech was postponed, giving him enough time to research the style of other speeches and develop his own contribution.

Back in Port Pirie, the Frome electorate office in Ellen Centre, previously used by retiring MP Rob Kerin, was a near-empty shell. Geoff Brock surmises that the electoral records had been shredded or removed. There was only an old desk that looked as though it came from the 1960s, a couple of chairs, a television with a wire antenna and no pens or paper.

The first constituent with an issue was soon on the telephone. Robert Hosking of Narridy wanted to talk to Geoff about effluent disposal at Fisherman Bay. Sitting in the humble and basic surroundings of his new office, Geoff Brock was off and running as the new Independent Member for Frome.

Chapter 9

Listening Posts

Port Pirie was proclaimed the first provincial city in South Australia and was once the fourth-busiest port in Australia. These facts were mentioned by Geoff Brock in his maiden speech as Independent Member for Frome to the House of Assembly on 3 March 2009 (which can be read in Appendix A).

Mr Brock had begun his speech by saying he had been a mayor 'so I expect a bit of heckling'.

'I admit that, being in my third sitting week in parliament, I am still finding it a bit daunting. I am still finding my way around the corridors but I have found the canteen and toilets,' he said.

After members interjected, the speech continued. Geoff proudly said that Port Pirie once hosted three rail gauges and that trains traversing Australia needed to stop there to transfer passengers, goods and freight before continuing their journeys.

> *There were three major oil company installations with large bulk storage tanks for the various petroleum products, a large maritime and stevedoring industry, a Coca-Cola bottling plant, bread and cake factories and during World War II the local aerodrome served as a training facility for more than 4000 pilots from around Australia.*

Port Pirie is rebirthing itself and the optimism is tremendous throughout the community and region, and it is working towards becoming a retail commercial service outlet for the north. The second-largest location is Clare, which is a great tourist destination, with the main employment being derived from tourism, sheep, beef cattle and grain growing and its vineyards and great quality wines.

Geoff Brock set about harnessing the energy of his far-flung electorate after his stunning success at the 2009 by-election. It may not have been 'campaigning' in the true sense of the word, but he was on the hustings. Through a series of uniquely named 'listening posts' in the towns of the Frome electorate, he gained insight into the needs of the people. Everything from the leaky roof at the bowls club to the state of the kitchen in the Institute Hall was discussed.

Geoff Brock hired halls at such places as Tarlee, Marrabel, Manoora, Riverton, Clare, Gladstone, Laura, Port Broughton, Bute and Snowtown. After advertising his visit in the local newspaper, he pulled up a chair and notepad . . . and waited.

'There is "listening" and there is "listening",' Geoff said.

I went to areas that I had not visited for many, many years. I talked to organisations and businesses. The aim was to get out there to understand issues outside the Port Pirie Regional Council area. I had no idea what the issues were in the Clare Valley, Barunga West or Gladstone and Laura, but I began by going out there every day of the week. People could visit me for two hours at the listening posts and avoid travelling distances up to 100 kilometres to reach me in Port Pirie.

I am still doing it today. I received invitations to speak at events as the new member. I would speak to progress associations and councils, bearing in mind I had just 12 months before the next election in 2010. In that time, I covered 120,000 kilometres and went through two government-lease cars. I expected to encounter the two preselected candidates for the major parties in my travels, but I didn't see them until two or three months before the next election.

Someone said I would go to the opening of a postage stamp. I was doing what I considered a politician should do and that is being out there with the people. My presence out there in the first 12 months increased my profile in the wider community. Some people might say it was campaigning, but in my mind I was doing my job.

Geoff spoke about one visit in particular.

I was at Tarlee for a meeting and gave an overview of my life's journey, warts and all. Afterwards, people told me they never thought they would hear a politician being so open about their personal life and tragedies.

I don't want to say I am respected out there because that is not the word. I hope I can relate to people who may have been in the same position as I was early in life. There are people out there who don't like me and that is just the nature of the game; I expect that.

My philosophy has been to really listen to people.

Many of the people taking part in the listening posts were volunteers from all walks of life . . . and Geoff Brock considers himself to be one of them despite his salary.

'I have been volunteering in some capacity for the past 37 years since we came back to Port Pirie from Port Augusta; I understand the value of volunteering,' he said. 'Some people in positions of power don't go the extra mile, but I believe in serving the people who support me as well as looking after those who may not have supported me.'

While there was straight talking and loads of community involvement in the country, Geoff was frustrated by the double-dealing in Parliament House.

In the first week after taking office, he lobbed a query about 'super schools' at Education Minister Jane Lomax-Smith in question time in the House of Assembly. It was his first experience of question time, a session when backbenchers can quiz state government ministers. He asked about the direction of the super school issue, bearing in mind that many Port Pirie residents opposed such a merger of primary and secondary campuses. There was no time limit in those days on responses to questions without notice and Mr Brock listened intently as the minister waffled for many minutes.

'I look forward to working closely with the Member for Frome,' the minister concluded to the bewildered newcomer MP. Geoff Brock tried to understand her response before seeking a copy of Hansard to confirm that she did not answer the question.

'I remember it so vividly. She went right around the question and her response did not satisfy my requirements,' he said.

Geoff Brock then invited Dr Lomax-Smith to Port Pirie to speak to residents involved with the primary and secondary schools and discuss the government's proposal for a super school. After returning from a tour of the north, she attended a community meeting in the Frome electorate office during a long weekend. Dr Lomax-Smith noted the concerns that were expressed and took the super school in Port Pirie off the agenda. 'She indicated it was up to the community to decide the issue,' Geoff said. It was Geoff Brock's first success story as a parliamentarian.

'I congratulated the people from the various schools who had come into my office at the weekend,' he said. 'This kind of success doesn't happen every day, but when it does, it is sweet.'

It was not such smooth sailing when Geoff Brock stepped up for a research trip to China in 2009. Amid criticism that his 10-day trip was a 'holiday', he travelled to Shandong Province, Shanghai and Beijing to look at renewable energy, wind farms and aquaculture. The trip resulted from a long-standing invitation received when he was Port Pirie mayor.

Chapter 10

Speaker of the House?

With the 2010 state election rapidly approaching, Geoff Brock called together his old campaign team, with a few new faces, to plan his strategy. Over a few drinks, a plan began to develop. They would put up corflute signs and banners left over from the 2009 campaign as well as wear T-shirts and caps. Geoff Brock would once again contribute about $10,000 towards his re-election.

He arranged with Southern Cross Television's Joby Connor to make a television commercial on a tight budget. The commercial featured Mr Brock holding placards that featured pictures of the local Labor and Liberal candidates with their leaders' images on the reverse side. He flipped the placards and pointed out who voters would really be supporting with their vote. He then said those who voted for him would be supporting him only and would gain his undivided attention. The 15-second promotion, costing $1000, won the Best Political Advertisement Award in a competition organised by the *Advertiser* website AdelaideNow.

In 2014, local Labor Party loyalists were stunned to learn that Mr Weatherill was unable to remember the name of then Labor candidate for the seat, Marcus Connelly. The late Mr Connelly was a nephew of a previous local Independent Labor MP, the late Ted Connelly, who had lost Labor preselection, then won the seat as an Independent Labor Member. He had given his crucial vote to the Dunstan government, then later rejoined the Labor Party.

Mr Weatherill had his embarrassing memory lapse when visiting the Country Fire Service brigade in Crystal Brook and the media was there to record it. The seeming lack of respect for Frome Labor contenders had been evident in 2010 when the then Labor premier Mike Rann opened a wind farm at Clements Gap, near Redhill. The Labor candidate at the time, John Rohde, was absent from the ceremony. Mr Rohde was campaigning for the state election under the Country Labor banner, but it was Geoff Brock who stood with Mike Rann in a photograph of the opening ceremony published in the *Recorder* on 23 February 2010.

The $120 million wind farm was the first project in South Australia by owner Pacific Hydro. Generating almost 57 megawatts, the site could power 30,000 homes every year. Premier Rann was quoted in the newspaper as saying it was a 'terrific new chapter in an ongoing story'.

'We have more wind power than any other state,' he said, naturally oblivious to the controversy that would surround SA's renewable-energy policy only a few years later. He said the state would meet a target of providing 20 per cent of its energy from renewables seven years earlier than projected, and added: 'We will match California's target of having 33 per cent in renewable energy. This will put us in an international leadership position.'

In the weeks before Mr Rann's visits in 2010, the Liberals had been courting the votes of Port Pirie residents. Opposition leader Isobel Redmond arrived in the city offering more than $2 million for two projects. She promised that the Liberals, if elected, would contribute the money towards a recycled water project and a hearty $250,000 for a new Meals on Wheels kitchen.

'Port Pirie relies almost totally on the River Murray via one pipeline. This exposes the vulnerability of the town's water security,' the leader said. 'The Liberal Party has been lobbying the state and federal governments to work together with the Port Pirie Regional Council and Nyrstar to address the city's water supply issues.' Ms Redmond strolled the main street with Frome Liberal candidate Terry Boylan, posing for a photograph with sales assistant Gabby Benstead at a clothes rack outside a fashion store. If the Liberal party had been successful at the election, Isobel Remond would have become our state's first woman premier.

In a light-hearted piece, the *Recorder* contrasted the leader's up-to-the-moment appearance with her comment that she was once a 'dinosaur'. She was referring to her previous role as a general lawyer handling everything from Family Court matters to native title claims to litigation over faulty breast implants.

'I call myself a "dinosaur" because we were a dying breed as sole practitioners in general practice', she said. 'I did whatever cases came through the door. In family law cases, I found it fairly sad that people who once said they loved each other were squabbling over the laundry basket.'

A few days before the 2010 election, Geoff Brock pledged to ask the people for guidance if he held the balance of power with other Independents. (In fact, the scenario of his holding the sole deciding vote eventuated after the subsequent poll four years later.) At the time he pledged to call meetings in Port Pirie, Clare and Gladstone to assess voters' opinions in the wake of the 2010 election. He said he would have 'vigorous' talks with both Labor leader Mr Rann and the Liberals' Ms Redmond.

'I will look for what they can give Frome,' he said, offering a hint of what was to come in his future dealings with Mr Weatherill.

On polling day in March 2010, Geoff Brock's Liberal rival Terry Boylan was photographed at the Risdon Park Primary School polling booth with his wife Denise and daughter Georgia, who had voted for the first time. Although Georgia was coy about who she supported, informed political sources suggested it was her dad.

'I can't say who I voted for. A vote is a bit of a personal thing,' she told the *Recorder*. 'I think my dad would be good at whatever he does.'

In a welcome sign for his supporters, Geoff Brock had arranged for how-to-vote cards to be distributed at all 27 booths rather than the seven that were manned in 2009. On poll day, 20 March, he voted at the Baptist Church, then visited all polling booths before returning to face the media at his home, which had been again invaded by a television station's satellite dish on the front lawn.

By 9 pm, the election-night party was in full swing with loud cheers every time there was an update on the voting numbers for Mr Brock.

'I woke next morning and was cleaning up the mess when I had a call from Premier Mike Rann,' he recalled. With postal, absentee and pre-poll votes still to be counted, the supremely confident Mr Rann had a suggestion. He offered the role of Speaker of the House of Assembly to a surprised Geoff Brock. Mr Rann was under no compulsion to make the offer with the Labor government about to be declared re-elected and Mr Brock not holding the balance of power.

'I was taken aback. Mike said I would be a good choice. The premier had been under pressure over the Chantelois case, in which an irate estranged husband attacked Mr Rann at the Adelaide Wine Centre,' Geoff Brock said.

There were whispers among the media about my being a candidate for the Speaker's role and finally Mike confirmed to reporters that he had offered the position to me.

He had been pussyfooting around before that and I assume he confirmed the offer to be upfront with the media because his credibility was being questioned by the other controversy. He was on the phone to me within 30 seconds to say he had mentioned the offer.

Geoff Brock revealed he had reservations.

I didn't have the political experience to be the Speaker and, more important, I had been elected for only 12 months and didn't feel I fully understood the issues in the electorate.

I had calls from previous Speakers, offering conflicting advice. They included Graham Gunn and John Trainer plus other retired MPs. I was contacted by Member for Giles Lyn Breuer, based at Whyalla, who was to be the Deputy Speaker. She urged me to accept the position and suggested that because of her experience, she would perform some of the duties away from parliamentary sitting days to enable me to continue being an effective member in my electorate.

Mike started ringing me every day to ask what I was doing. I would have earned an extra $100,000, had special staff and a government car and driver who would take me to and from Adelaide. As attractive as it was, after discussions with my partner Lyn Akker, I decided against taking the position. The premier was disappointed, but accepted my decision. He didn't have to give me anything because he could govern in his own right.

If I had taken that role, and neglected the voters in my electorate because of a lack of time, I might not have been re-elected in 2014 and had the balance-of-power position to help Nyrstar to facilitate the future success of the smelters and Port Pirie.

It all went back to my decision to resign from the smelters, to step down as mayor, to run for Frome as an Independent and the 30 votes that put me into a winning position in the preference count in the 2009 by-election. The stars had aligned for me to have a role in the future security of Port Pirie's largest employer and the prospects for families in Port Pirie and surrounding locations with the transformation of the smelters.

In a front-page report headlined 'Old Brock Magic' the *Recorder* told how Geoff Brock had blitzed his rivals at the poll with a dramatic vote rise. He scraped into the seat at the 2009 by-election, but now an incredible extra 3408 voters had backed him into the 2010 title. This was a 75 per cent increase on his previous share of ballots. He was eventually declared winner by 3159 votes ahead of his old rival, the Liberals' Terry Boylan.

Many of Mr Brock's new votes came from the country. His listening post strategy had paid off with huge increases in his vote at booths such as Blyth, Georgetown, Marrabel, Brinkworth, Watervale, Yacka and Clare.

Support also rose at booths in Port Pirie. Meanwhile, Terry Boylan's share of ballots increased by two per cent while John Rohde's declined by 23 per cent. Mr Boylan declined to confirm his intention to continue as a candidate while Mr Rohde, who grew up in the Whitlam and Dunstan Labor eras, stepped down, saying it was time to hand on the baton to a fresh contender.

'Premier Mr Rann highlighted a need to reconnect with the country regions and I hope that can be a party priority,' he said. 'I congratulate Mr Brock on his commitment to the role in the next four years.' John Rohde later told journalist Dylan Smith that he had been passionate about Labor when just a boy in Marrabel.

'I grew up in the 1970s under a Whitlam and Dunstan team. My brother was enlisted to go to Vietnam, but this was scrapped under the Whitlam government. I remember sitting in my classroom in 1975 when they announced over the speaker that Prime Minister Whitlam had been sacked. I was disappointed, but my classmates did not understand the concept,' he said.

Chapter 11

Of Life and Death

Death threats and a suicidal thought lay behind the glittering prize of Geoff Brock's success. He had become the Independent Member for Frome and was now a Cabinet minister in the Weatherill government. The down-to-earth politician had been re-elected in a landslide at the 2010 state election amid a wave of popularity. Privately, he endured some personal challenges in the following years, but kept up a strong public face.

Then, after the 2014 poll, he shaped the South Australian government using his balance-of-power status and was invited to become Regional Development Minister and Local Government Minister. He had the world at his feet. Few people knew that he had, indeed, been offered the same portfolios by a Liberal government, if it were elected.

Despite the glory, Geoff Brock was plagued by negativity from some residents and severely questioned his own self-worth. After his re-election in 2010, Geoff continued to greet residents who called at his office in Ellen Centre, Port Pirie. His staff offer cups of tea and coffee to people who are sometimes agitated about an issue.

'Most people who come into the office to raise issues with their local MP are frustrated because they don't know what to do and they want answers,' Geoff said.

I sit them down and listen. Obviously there are some people I can't accommodate. On one occasion, a guy was yelling and screaming at the staff. The staff, sheltering behind security glass, were terrified. They retreated and he walked out. I made it clear that I would not tolerate any physical or verbal abuse towards my staff or family so I reported it to the police.

On another occasion, I was in parliament and the unsuccessful Frome Labor candidate John Rohde had a phone call in which he was abused verbally by a caller who said he was going to parliament to 'get that Brock'. John rang and told me what was happening and phoned the parliament security services who had a photograph of the offender and were ready to stop him if he entered the building.

The same person had been making verbal threats against my partner Lyn Akker, leaving abusive and vile messages on our phones. We approached a magistrate who issued a restraining order to keep the man from being within a certain distance of me, my family and my home. He had been agitated over a political issue dating back to when I was mayor.

On yet another occasion, Geoff Brock was forced to activate an alarm when a person yelled and screamed at electorate office staff. Two police officers came to the rescue.

'Usually, the behaviour of constituents is exemplary – there would be thousands who visit the office,' he said.

As a result of the incidents, a sign was put in the window warning that police were monitoring the site. As well, a police car was parked nearby for several weeks to deter troublemakers. In addition, police vehicles frequently travelled past the office for the next few weeks as an extra precaution.

But that did not stop Geoff from receiving two hip-and-shoulder bumps from unhappy foes. The first came after he voted with the state government to protect marine parks legislation in parliament in November 2014. The decision was carried by one vote – his.

'The sanctuary zones had been in force for two years and the legislation was now being passed to put it into law,' Geoff Brock said.

The pressure was on me as Regional Development Minister to get rid of the zones. But I wonder what the local MPs in those areas were doing about the matter in those ensuing two years to reflect the wishes of their communities? It was all being laid at my doorstep.

On the day of the vote in parliament, the gallery was packed with people for and against the legislation. When I had to make my call to speak, I was shaking, emotional and scared. I had to make a choice about a decision that was made two years previously. The local MPs who opposed it should have been fighting the government during this time.

The other Independent, Martin Hamilton-Smith, voted with the Opposition to get rid of about 16 of the 79 sanctuary zones. I voted with the government and sanctuary zones were introduced with my casting vote. When I crossed the floor to vote against the Opposition's motion, it was very emotional. I received 'death' stares and people were muttering 'traitor'.

While Geoff was standing on the Opposition side of the House, one of the local MPs whose electorate was affected by the legislation – Liberal MP for Finniss, Michael Pengilly – allegedly bumped him, almost knocking him over.

'He gave me a hip-and-shoulder and threw me off balance and it was captured on the Channel 7 news video,' Geoff said.

> *Fisheries Minister Leon Bignell asked Speaker Michael Atkinson to rule that someone had been assaulted. The Speaker asked me whether I had been assaulted. Of course I had been assaulted and had fallen into another MP standing nearby, which prevented me from falling to the floor.*
>
> *I replied to the Speaker that it had been an emotional day and I did not want to comment about what had happened in the debate. If I had spoken up, that member may have been barred from parliament for assault.*

At the time, the *Recorder* in Port Pirie reported:

> *Regional Development Minister Geoff Brock may have been pushed by a rival MP in parliament, but no knockout punch was landed against him . . .*
>
> *Mr Pengilly responded to a text from the* Recorder. *He was asked whether he had hip-and-shouldered Mr Brock and sworn at him. 'No, I did not. I actually heard the alleged comment as well!' he said. 'Given that I have a new hip, the other is a joke. I pushed past him to get to my seat as he was standing by the entrance.'*
>
> *Mr Brock said he had listened to locals before casting his vote. 'I didn't support the Bill because their proposals had the potential to seriously undermine the effectiveness of the marine parks network and undo much of the good work that has been done during a decade,' he said. 'The time has come to take the politics out of this issue and focus more clearly on exploring the potential of our regional areas.'*

Jeff Sutton, an amateur fisherman based at Balaklava and spokesman for Marine Park 14 Action Group, clashed with Geoff Brock over the marine park legislation. Mr Sutton said about seven professional fishermen based at Port Wakefield were 'going broke' because of the laws restricting fishing.

'Mr Brock is pretty well on the nose, but I will preface that by saying I voted for him and I wish I had not done so,' he said.

> *He said in a speech that was videotaped that he would help with marine parks, but, when it came to the crunch, he didn't. Mr Weatherill bought and sold him. He got millions of dollars for the northern regions . . . but in the end he sold his soul.*

Mr Sutton said he would not vote for Mr Brock again.

'He would agree that I was the first person at a public meeting at the bowling club in Balaklava who said he could well have the balance-of-power,' he said. 'He just looked at me and laughed.'

Jeff Sutton was not the only one unhappy with Geoff Brock at this time. Geoff had received death threats on the phone with callers warning there was a 'bullet for him' and he should 'watch the back' of his head.

But not every protestor had sinister intent. Late on a Sunday evening, the landline phone at his office rang and the caller was surprised that Geoff was still at work. The male caller quizzed him about his decision on sanctuary zones and listened as Geoff explained his motives. The man then said he had 'never thought of that' and they parted on good terms.

But things could still get physical, as Geoff found at the 2015 Spencer Gulf League football grand final at Memorial Oval in Port Pirie when he saw a cliffhanger win to Solomontown against West

Augusta. As he was heading to the change rooms to congratulate the Cats' coach Chris Pollard, a retired footballer broke ranks with the crowd, targeting the small-statured politician. Yelling obscenities, the assailant delivered a hip-and-shoulder bump against him. The impact threw Geoff into an elderly lady in the crowd.

'He was a big solid boy and I knew him, but he no longer lived in my electorate. It was just after the marine park legislation vote so I can only surmise that triggered the attack,' he said. 'That is the ugly side of politics. Actions like that tarnish the 99 per cent of people who accept the democratic system.'

Geoff Brock said he and his partner Lyn had felt tense in the wake of the threats and attacks.

'While Lyn didn't say anything to me, I know from discussions later, she feared for my physical and mental well-being,' he said.

> *I am a sensitive person and I certainly don't like conflict. I would rather there be a discussion about an issue with everyone still having respect for each other. Lyn was anxious and it affected my children and grandchildren. The grandchildren would phone me, especially if I was away, to check that I was okay.*
>
> *It was a by-product of the media frenzy about this legislation. You could not get the true facts out there. I know the media has a role to play, but at the same time they should be looking at the ongoing effects. We may be politicians, but we are people. I think the public sometimes doesn't see that, just as they don't see sportspeople as real people.*
>
> *We see footballers on television and say, 'Why did he do that?' but they are still people trying to do their best. They may*

be physically exhausted or have some injury, but we don't see that.

Politicians want to solve the world's problems, but at times I would come home and think, Is this all worth it? I took it personally. It affected my sleeping habits. I was looking over my shoulder for a time. Was someone going to king-hit me?

As the tension ratcheted up, Geoff Brock began to contemplate his future.

'You need to have confidence in yourself. With the abuse and death threats, it makes you stop and think, Should I just walk in front of a car? You wonder whether it is worth going on,' he said.

You ask whether you should be doing this, whether you are the best person for the role or whether you should quit. That is the downside. While these questions are in the back of your mind, they sap your confidence. You wonder whether you have the community on your side and it makes it hard to go that extra step.

Quite often when I was away in Adelaide, I had thoughts about whether I should carry on. But then I thought about my family. If I had a serious injury or didn't carry on, what about the people who believe in me and encourage me? How would I be seen in their eyes?

I needed a reality check. I had to make up my mind that I was not going to take this and to rise above it. Some politicians may not show it, but it is a hard game. You try not to show that emotion and the impact some of these things have on you personally or emotionally. We have to put up a facade and not show the people we are wavering.

In 2010, Geoff Brock's strength of character and personality were tested to the maximum. There were two tragedies in his family, which will have an everlasting effect on many people. Despite opening up on many other issues he has requested privacy here.

'We are still trying to recover from this,' he said. 'It will be with us for the rest of our lives.'

Not surprisingly, Geoff Brock believes parliamentarians should make their decisions with honesty, compassion and knowledge. They should also take the 'long' view of the impact of those resolutions. Some benefits eventuate after the politician has stepped down from office.

'We see decisions being made by one side of politics . . . rather than asking whether this action can be improved upon by going in another direction, or by discussing it,' he said.

It has got to the stage in Australia that there is public negativity about everything we are doing. We are not getting anywhere. We should be sitting down and working out the best opportunities and suggestions from either side.

I see problems on both sides of politics at federal and state level around Australia. People are becoming sick of the blame game and are looking for a solution to the issues facing our nation. The media too often portrays the negative side instead of talking about the challenges and what is really happening on the ground. Too often we don't hear about the progress being made.

It is a dirty game, but I enjoy it. You need a thick hide. My community doesn't owe me anything nor does this state or country – I owe these people. I want to be able to look back and say, 'I had a shot at that.'

I am only 68 and I am not ready to retire – who knows what will happen at the 2018 state election? I have lots of ideas I want to continue pushing. There is no way I can do nothing.

Chapter 12

Who Created the Kingmaker?

Was Geoff Brock, the Independent powerbroker, actually created by the Liberals? One school of thought is that the Liberal Party concentrated on toppling the three Independents – Geoff Brock, Bob Such and Don Pegler – to their detriment of winning marginal city-based Labor seats at the 2014 state election.

The argument put forward by some observers is that when two of the Independents – Brock and Such – were returned, and the Liberals failed to pick up marginal city-based Labor seats, they lacked the number of seats needed to bring about a scenario in which Geoff Brock would have supported a minority Liberal government instead of a minority Labor administration.

'They may have created my kingmaker role,' Geoff Brock said. 'My priority was that the state have stable government. It turned out that the Liberals would not have been able to form government, even if I had supported them. If they had won one or two marginal seats, the situation could well have been reversed.'

Other commentators believe Geoff Brock was predetermined to back Labor into office and nothing would change that. Associate Professor Wayne Errington, of the University of Adelaide's politics and international studies department, agrees with the notion that Geoff's crucial role was a by-product of the Liberals' election strategy. 'It came back to haunt them,' he said.

The Liberals could have gone harder against Geoff Brock in 2014. A retired Liberal MP said a proposed strong political attack against Geoff had never eventuated. He said Geoff had not been targeted to any great extent in the electorate, explaining that local party members had wanted to paint him as being a 'vote for Labor', but it was feared that this was too extreme.

The ex-politician said he had predicted Geoff Brock would win the balance of power and side with Labor. 'I cannot endorse or criticise Mr Brock now because we have to win that seat in 2018,' he said.

> *He is a community person. He was thrust into parliament. He was always going to have the balance-of-power and was always going to support Labor. That reflects on him and he is tarnished as a result.*
>
> *The state government has lost the plot regarding electricity prices and everything else. Mr Brock is a nice enough man, he is diligent, he tries. I cannot say he is a hero because we have to work hard to see him retire from politics.*

Meanwhile, Associate Professor Errington said Geoff Brock was now in the unusual situation of being an Independent MP sitting in Cabinet. He said Geoff was obviously popular and had a typical Independent's background in local government. His ascendancy to office in 2009 was achieved in trademark maverick style.

'Winning in a by-election is not unusual because people can vote for an Independent without changing the government,' Wayne Errington said. 'Independents will come and go over local issues without a whole lot of consequence. They are seen as having integrity because they don't have to take any tough votes.'

Associate Professor Errington was asked whether Geoff Brock had been in the right place at the right time.

'Or the wrong place, depending on your point of view,' he replied.

He said the Liberals had failed to use their campaign resources throughout the state in the best possible way.

'You don't alienate the Independents and you seek to win marginal seats from Labor,' he said. He had predicted Mr Brock would be re-elected comfortably in 2014 and said he was likely to win again in 2018.

Another political commentator, Emeritus Professor Dean Jaensch of Flinders University, was less complimentary about the man from Port Pirie.

'Mr Brock has been the absent minister in this government,' he said. 'He just doesn't have a public face at all.' But he praised Geoff's 'political acumen' for achieving the Nyrstar smelter deal.

'It was what the government wanted to happen, you could say,' he said. 'It would be fair to give him credit for that.'

He attributed Geoff's support for the then-minority Labor government to the 'cleverness and cunning' of Premier Jay Weatherill, who travelled to Port Pirie to win over the re-elected Independent.

'Everything is up for challenge in 2018,' said Emeritus Professor Jaensch. He said Jay Weatherill and Opposition leader Steven Marshall were neck-and-neck in opinion polls and Geoff Brock was 'vulnerable to a challenge'.

'It depends whether the Liberal Party has a candidate who really connects with the electorate,' he said.

The same could be said for the future Labor candidate for the seat – or would this contender purely provide preferences for Geoff? With Labor likely to finish behind Geoff Brock and the Liberals in primary votes, the preferences would be crucial. Traditionally, the Labor preferences strongly favour Geoff, who, like Labor candidate John Rohde, includes Gough Whitlam among his political heroes.

While less formidable than Mr Whitlam, South Australia's two major party leaders will to a large extent shape the outcome in Frome in 2018. Jay Weatherill, a quietly combative premier, is expected to be up against the now battle-hardened Steven Marshall in the contest for votes. Some see the coming election as a verdict on an increasingly under-siege Labor administration and a Liberal team yet to prove itself.

Professor of Politics at Flinders University, Haydon Manning, said Geoff could find it 'really difficult' to retain his seat in 2018, but Mr Marshall would have to first persuade voters that he is a viable alternative. He said Geoff's future was 'tagged with the government'.

In 2014, the Independent MP had the good fortune of playing the role of kingmaker with leverage 'far, far more than that of a backbencher', the professor said. 'The danger of taking on more responsibility and making more decisions is that you upset more people and you become more closely identified with the government,' he said.

He conceded that Nationals MP Karlene Maywald and former Liberal Rory McEwen had gained swings toward them after becoming Independents in recent SA history, despite their being connected to the Rann government of the era.

'Independents who join Cabinet are not doomed,' he said. 'If you are a kingmaker or queenmaker, you can do a lot. The dilemma will be that the voters like you, but they don't like the government and that over-rides the "like" for you when they want to change the government.'

Professor Manning agreed that the Liberals had targeted the Independents, particularly the late Dr Bob Such, at the 2014 election. 'There is an argument that they foolishly targeted Dr Such too much,' he said. 'I can understand them targeting Frome because it is a traditional Liberal seat.'

He agreed that by not winning marginal Labor-held city seats, and directing futile action against the Independents, the Liberals had created Geoff Brock as kingmaker.

The outcome of the poll, both statewide and locally, will hinge on whether people believe Mr Marshall would be a 'half-decent premier' and would lead a team of 'half-decent ministers'.

If Steven Marshall falters, Geoff Brock and the Nick Xenophon-led SA Best would step into the breach in Frome and various other seats.

On the other hand, Steven Marshall, if elected, could face SA Best putting a 'brake' on his new administration, according to the professor. That new administration could include Kendall Jackson who, as the Liberal candidate, is taking up the fight to Geoff Brock in Frome with a series of strong local issues.

Geoff with his father, Ian Brock, at Frankston in Victoria in 1950.

Mary, left, Geoff, Peter, Ian and Keith Brock with baby Lynda in the stroller in 1964.

Geoff, right, was the lucky one to be wearing a school blazer in this photograph with his brothers Peter, left, and Ian in 1964.

In 1967, Geoff had bought his first corduroy jacket and trousers with his own money, thinking he was 'top dog'.

Geoff cutting the cake at his 21st birthday in 1971.

Geoff at his 21st being congratulated by his father, Ian, at their housing trust home in Barry Street in 1971.

Geoff Brock with his late wife Arlene at a social event.

At the helm of an armoured personnel carrier during Army Reserve manoeuvres at El Elamein, near Whyalla, in 1972.

The roadhouse at Port Augusta that was operated by Geoff Brock in the 1970s.

In 1993, Geoff's daughter Hayley, second from right, won a school essay competition on the subject of federal government. She was congratulated by South Australian Labor Senator Nick Bolkus, left, student Jasmine Anderson, and local Labor figure Barry Piltz.

Geoff Brock posed for this photograph outside the Member for Frome's office in Port Pirie in 2008. He was elected to office for the first time the following year.

Labor Attorney-General Michael Atkinson, later speaker of the House of Assembly, with Jennifer Rankine at the Blessing of the Fleet ball in Port Pirie. In a conversation at the ball, Mr Atkinson urged Geoff Brock to run as an Independent.

Lyn Akker and Geoff Brock celebrate Geoff's first election win in 2009 at their home in Port Pirie.

Premier Jay Weatherill and Geoff Brock sign the $291 million loan guarantee agreement in the Nyrstar boardroom in Port Pirie in 2014.

Geoff shares a light-hearted moment with Prince Charles during their visit to Seppeltsfield Winery in the Barossa Valley in 2016.

Geoff is about to swallow a scorpion, a traditional dish, while dining with the Linyi Mayor and delegation member and Salisbury Mayor Gillian Aldridge during his China trip in 2016.

South Australia and Shandong Provin celebrated the 30th anniversary of the sister-state relationship in 2016. Here Geoff chats to an interpreter at the waterfront in Linyi, China, while visiti with a local government delegation.

Almonds alive . . . state Liberal MP Adrian Pederick, left, Geoff Brock, Michael Costa and federal Liberal MP Tony Pasin celebrate at the Costa Brothers processing plant in Swan Reach in 2017.

The Independent Member for Frome is about to toss the coin before a soccer final in Port Pirie in 2017.

During the Country Cabinet meeting in Port Pirie in 2017, Hiltje Hulsinga and Geoff Brock chat about plans for an access mat for disabled people at the beach.

Lincoln McKenzie-Landers, five, and his sister Willow, five, met Geoff outside a Port Pirie store in 2017.

Lining up for a snag at the Lions Club of Port Pirie barbecue outside a retail centre in Port Pirie in 2017. Geoff is with Domenic Caputo, second from left, George Rajkovic, Andrew Patterson and Dylan Smith.

With the 'hot commissioning' of the Nyrstar redevelopment only months away, Geoff Brock visited the plant in 2017.

Chapter 13

Six Months to Live

Geoff Brock triumphed in 2014 despite having been given just six months to live when diagnosed with prostate cancer. About 12 months earlier, he had experienced abdominal pain while having coffee with some Liberal MPs, Mount Gambier Independent Don Pegler and Independent Bob Such in Parliament House. After seeking leave from parliament, he drove himself home to Port Pirie where he was admitted to hospital and treated for diverticulitis and given intravenous fluids before being discharged.

While in hospital he was asked why he had not followed up on a prostate-test referral from five years previously and he was referred to another urologist. 'As a lot of males do, I shrugged it off. I had no symptoms and was being referred only because of my age,' Geoff recalled, but he saw the urologist and later had a blood test. With a Prostate Specific Antigen (PSA) result of 2, 'everything was fine' – or so he thought. He was given an internal examination and ordered to have a CAT scan.

Bad news was waiting for Geoff when he saw the urologist at his clinic in Adelaide.

> *The urologist told me it wasn't looking good. He showed me the scan and pointed to what he said were grey areas. I couldn't see a thing. I asked how bad it was and he replied it*

was significant. Again he showed me the dark images on the scans, but I couldn't see them.

When I asked again how bad it was he said it would 'probably be six months'.

'Six months for what . . . to live?'

'Yes,' he replied.

As despondency settled over the shocked grandfather, the urologist ordered an MRI scan.

'I drove home to Port Pirie thinking I may have six months to live and my mind was churning,' he said.

I thought I had had lots of opportunities in my life and I had seen and done many things. But my mind kept going back to when my children had lost their mother Arlene in the car accident. I was now thinking they might lose their father to cancer. When I returned to the house, Lyn could see something was distressing me. We had a chat and she became upset. We decided not to tell my children or grandchildren about the results.

Two weeks later, I had my MRI scan. I had kept busy and tried not to think about the situation, but it was always with me. I didn't want to add to the tragedy for my children. They had lost their mother and we had other personal tragedies. The impact of another loss would have been catastrophic.

But fate was on his side. When Geoff returned to see the urologist he was told, 'It's all looking good.' The scan had revealed the cancer was not as serious as first anticipated. Words could not describe his relief when told the news.

He also found solace from fellow Independent Dr Bob Such, who had survived prostate cancer and was a great supporter of modern robotic techniques for removal of this kind of malignancy. After a successful operation to remove his prostate gland, Geoff Brock had his urinary catheter removed by a medical attendant who turned out to have family connections to Port Pirie.

'I was clenching my fingers on the bed and closing my eyes, expecting pain, but she had taken it out seconds earlier. She did a terrific job,' he said.

Despite the uncertainty about his health, Geoff Brock never doubted that he would contest the 2014 election.

'I had learned a lot, particularly about representing voters' concerns by going directly to the ministers concerned instead of sounding off in an uninformed way,' he said.

> *It was ingrained in me when I worked at the smelters – if you go head-to-head, no one wants to back off. This was also my experience in dealing with union officials. The more you argue, the less chance there is of resolving anything. Whoever has the purse strings is crucial to the discussion.*
>
> *I would use the same tactics with whichever party is in power because this is the side that controls the state's money.*

Supporters from both sides of the political spectrum helped Geoff Brock retain his seat in 2014. His team included six Labor supporters and eight 'blue Liberals'.

'The Liberals who supported me were disappointed that their party could not win very marginal seats. In some cases there were only one per cent margins. They felt they concentrated too much on challenging the Independents such as myself, Dr Such and Mr Pegler,' he said.

'Whether they voted for me is not the point – these people just appreciated what I tried to do for them as the local member.'

Once again the campaign was run on a minimal budget. One pensioner called into the electoral office to offer a $10 donation, saying, 'You need it more than me.'

But something was in the wind – on election day, the small band of supporters was overwhelmed at the polling booths and exhausted their supply of how-to-vote cards. More had to be printed on the day. The result was known by 7 pm amid the usual blur of election eve for Geoff Brock.

Early next morning his mobile rang; Labor leader Jay Weatherill was on the line.

'The word going around political circles was that the Liberals would win the poll by two or three seats. When I saw Mr Weatherill's number come up on my phone, I wondered whether I should offer my commiserations on his defeat,' he said.

> *His first words were, 'We have to talk.' I asked him what we needed to talk about and he replied the voting for seats stood at 23–22 and Dr Such and I could determine the future government.*
>
> *I had a text message from Liberal leader Steven Marshall asking me to phone him. When I rang him, he said he wanted to talk about the future government and I told him that I had spoken to Mr Weatherill. I said I would talk to both leaders in Adelaide about what the future may hold.*

In one-to-one talks, both leaders offered Mr Brock the portfolios of Regional Development and Local Government in a new government in exchange for his support on the floor of the House of Assembly.

'I said I was astounded we were in this situation and they both explained what they would need to offer Dr Such and me to gain support to form government,' he said.

> *Despite the formalities and niceties, my priority was the Nyrstar transformation and I made that plain to both leaders. Both said they were talking to then Liberal prime minister Tony Abbott about a loan guarantee for the company. Mr Abbott was resolute that if a company was unable to stand on its own two feet, it should not go looking for government support. He was doing the same with the automotive industry and the SPC fruit business. I feared the worst. I needed assurance from the Commonwealth that there would be support for this, but it was not forthcoming.*

While climbing into buses or taxis in Adelaide during the top-level talks, Geoff was besieged by people urging him to support Liberal, or Labor. He then returned to Port Pirie to call in representatives of five councils in his area to gain an insight into their needs under a future government.

Meanwhile, Lyn had commented that Bob Such had slurred his words when he appeared on television. He then disappeared from the scene for a couple of days.

'Dr Such later rang me to say he had seen a doctor and needed to take some time off,' Geoff Brock said. Now back in Adelaide, Geoff pleaded with the media to give his colleague some respite. The Port Pirie-based politician was on the brink of exhaustion himself.

Channel 10 reporter Jane Stinson, who later became a Labor candidate, then broadcast emotive images from Port Pirie of

Geoff's family including his 18-month-old grandson Jax kissing his grandfather's image on television.

'Watching this, it came to mind that I needed to talk to my family and get guidance,' he said.

By this time, Dr Such had taken three months' leave-of-absence and had been taken out of the equation. I was receiving calls from Nyrstar in Switzerland just about every night, at 2 am or 3 am, to see whether there had been a decision on the future government. They were not concerned about which political party I supported. They just wanted a commitment for the European stock exchange on the loan guarantee proposal.

After Dr Such's announcement on the Saturday following the election, Mr Weatherill told me he was on his way to Port Pirie. Steven Marshall's people would have known the same thing about Dr Such, but I never had a phone call from the Liberals seeking to discuss the matter in Port Pirie.

After Mr Weatherill's government car pulled up outside Geoff Brock's house in Port Pirie, the premier joined his protégé for a cuppa under the pergola.

'I thought, he has got me over a barrel, but he led me to believe he was happy to consider the concessions that I was seeking,' Mr Brock recalled.

I feared he would have given me an ultimatum to support a stable government or they would go into caretaker mode. Before we got to this stage, I had asked both Mr Weatherill and Mr Marshall for a statement saying they were talking to Prime Minister Abbott about the Nyrstar loan guarantee proposal. I told both leaders that the European Stock Exchange needed a commitment.

Mr Weatherill gave me a letter saying that if the federal government failed to support the guarantee, then the Labor Party would do so if in government. I then gave that letter to Nyrstar management to satisfy the requirements in Europe. I told the media that we had an agreement.

Mr Marshall never provided a statement.

On top of providing the missing piece of the jigsaw in the Nyrstar transformation funding, Geoff Brock negotiated 57 concessions for Frome and regional areas from the premier. Dismissing the temptation to demand mega-millions for regional development, he sought $60 million over the four-year life of the parliament, plus $10 million extra funding for the first year. He then asked for more money for planning and development, tourism, and the Save The Murray campaign. Projects supported by the concessions included the multi-sport hub at Port Pirie, which won a $5 million grant.

In the four years, it added up to about $136 million plus the $291 million Nyrstar loan guarantee; all up a $427 million boost to regional South Australia, thanks to Geoff Brock's bargaining position.

'It was all thrashed out under my pergola with cups of coffee and tea and crackers with cheese,' he said. Mr Weatherill's adviser Simon Blewett, who also made the trip to Port Pirie, went to Mr Brock's electorate office for three-and-a-half hours' of two-finger typing to prepare a four-page agreement covering the concessions.

The premier watched the ABC television news at the house

before Geoff suggested pizza for dinner. Mr Weatherill and Mr Brock signed the document and, at around 10 pm, the premier headed back to Adelaide.

Next day, Mr Brock and Lyn travelled to Adelaide for him to sign a document supporting the Labor Party into government. Mr Weatherhill had earlier called Treasurer Tom Koutsantonis to tell him that Mr Brock was heading to Adelaide. The treasurer's first reaction was to wonder what would happen if Geoff Brock had a crash on the way to the city.

'I had tried to phone Mr Marshall to let him know that I was supporting Labor. I had to leave a message on his phone. I heard he was going to Canberra, but that he did not board the plane,' he said.

> *Ironically, Labor would have eventually formed government after winning Dr Such's seat in a by-election following Dr Such's death later in the year. I took lots of flak, but people are coming to me now saying that I only had one way to go in forming a government.*

He also had only one way to go in negotiating a deal to keep the smelter alive and help the people of Frome.

As former Labor Upper House President Ron Roberts, of Port Pirie, said: 'When you have them by the short and curlies, their hearts and minds will follow. You don't need to be smart. You just need a good grip.'

Chapter 14

'I Thought I Had it Tough'

As two diminutive men shook hands, it was hard not to think of the challenges both had faced so far in their lives. Governor Hieu Van Le, the Vietnamese refugee, was being congratulated by Geoff Brock, the boy who had grown up on the breadline. The occasion? Mr Le's swearing into vice-regal office at Government House in 2014.

As he grasped the Governor's hand, the new Weatherill government minister thought about how Mr Le had triumphed over danger in South Vietnam during the Vietnam War and survived a perilous boat journey to Australia, during which he was fired upon by Asian border patrols.

Geoff Brock was also keenly aware of his own success after growing up in a poor family at Wandearah, near Port Pirie. He was bullied at school and overcame a stutter. But Geoff admits his challenges paled in comparison to those faced by the Governor.

'I thought I had it tough, but it was nothing compared with Mr Le's life,' he said.

> *He is an example of an individual overcoming adversity to rise to high office in his adopted country. He is an inspiration. I can't reveal exactly what he said to me that day, but he congratulated me on my journey from the day of the election to holding the balance of power and entering the ministry.*

Geoff Brock, who had only recently become Regional Development Minister and Local Government Minister, had offices at 25 Grenfell Street in Adelaide and had been briefed on past and pending activities in both portfolios.

'There was no text book telling you what to do,' he recalled of his rise to administrative power.

It was only days after deciding who should govern. That was a pretty traumatic decision for a country lad to make. Within the first week of accepting my commission, I visited the regions, starting with Mount Gambier. My electorate was now the whole state. Every week I took the ministerial car to a region or, in the case of Mount Gambier, I flew there. The first person I met in Mount Gambier was a girl who said her father would like to talk to me.

I was introduced to her father, Dale Cleaves, who had been involved with the Generations In Jazz festival for many years with trumpeter James Morrison. He discussed the possibility of Morrison starting a jazz academy in the town. They wanted to have all the best jazz tutors come from around the world, especially the United States, to teach budding musicians.

It occurred to Geoff that this was pretty ambitious, but a business plan was submitted through the Department of Premier and Cabinet. The James Morrison Jazz Academy has now proven to be one of the greatest success stories in Mount Gambier with about 70 students and Morrison in residence.

It complemented the Generations In Jazz festival, which is held every year and attended by about 6500 people. The academy is attended by musicians from around Australia with a total participation of about 3500. It was something from 'outside the box', which is what I like to be involved in.

I had to be impartial in my dealings with Mr Cleaves, but originally and privately had my doubts about the project's success. I had never heard of Generations In Jazz, although it had been going for 20 years. The academy idea stacked up. No matter how wild something appears to be, there is always an opportunity for success. Every day we need to analyse what we are doing and listen to every possibility.

Geoff Brock and the Regional Development portfolio were a perfect match; he didn't want to be stuck in a city office, and the regions were desperate for attention. While travelling 360,000 kilometres in his car around the state, he aimed to speak to as many mayors and council chief executives as possible.

'I used to think it was extravagant to have a driver, but sometimes I attended five or six events in a day and it was helpful to be able to make phone calls and do paperwork in the backseat,' he said.

Wherever I went, people seemed to know who I was. This was great, but a little daunting. Many people felt as though they had previously been 'out of sight, out of mind'. I told them that they might be a fair distance away, but they were always in my mind.

With government support, he distributed grants under the $15 million Regional Development Fund. This was boosted by an extra $10 million in the first year after his successful lobbying of the treasurer, who freed up extra money for the seven Regional Development Australia agencies around the state. This meant an annual total of $3 million was available to them, compared with the original $1.4 million.

Negotiations took place with the chairman of the Regional Development Association, Rob Kerin, a former Liberal premier and Geoff Brock's predecessor as Frome MP. They had an excellent rapport, with the minister describing Mr Kerin as 'not political'.

'He is astute and has lots of experience in the region as a businessman, local politician, premier and grain industry figure,' Geoff said.

His knowledge and experience are greatly appreciated. There was no political manoeuvring. He just wanted to get on and do the best job he could for the regions. He is paid by Regional Development Australia, not the government.

With the Regional Development Fund in full flight, the government was doing its best to stimulate the rural economy. Stepping up the intensity, the government allocated almost $7 million more to fulfil the infrastructure and manufacturing projects initiated by the fund. In the years following the 2014 election, private investment in the regions hit almost $1 billion and more than 2000 jobs were created, all for a contribution of about $37 million by the state government.

'The rejuvenation defied the image of South Australia as a sprawling rust-bucket state,' said Geoff Brock.

As minister, he kept within touch of his far-flung constituents.

People have my phone number. Even the councils say they have a good relationship with me. We all know we are not going to get exactly what we want in negotiations. Trust is the biggest thing. If they don't trust you, that puts you behind the eight-ball.

Geoff Brock has faced some tumultuous times with the state's media, sometimes being targeted for his lack of polished political style. The *Recorder* newspaper at Port Pirie has published many reports and photographs in their coverage of his career. And despite being the first media outlet to become aware that Geoff planned to contest the 2009 by-election, the newspaper was lukewarm about his candidacy. More than once, editorials were published to highlight how the community would be aghast if he was elected as an Independent to then join one of the major political parties.

On the Thursday before the by-election, the *Recorder* published a front-page editorial urging readers to vote for Liberal candidate Terry Boylan. Geoff Brock took it on the chin and, to this day, refuses to gloat about how the then managing-editor got it wrong.

When he went on to win the 2010 and 2014 elections, the newspaper explored the reasons for his popularity. Local historian and former political adviser and broadcaster Andrew Male shared a story that he saw as representative of Geoff's appeal. He told the *Recorder* that an elderly couple had a problem with their footpath and when they called their MP he was at the door within 10 minutes wanting to help. Male believes:

> *Geoff Brock is just a humble, down-to-earth bloke . . . I have never known him to get bitter and twisted. Some people in politics say he shares a bit too much, but if I had to choose between someone who shares too much, or someone who locks himself in the car with the windows up, I would prefer Geoff Brock. He is the Bruce Springsteen of politics – he is doing these extraordinary things, but he still manages to come across as a normal guy.*

Chapter 15

Memories of a Small Man

With a sickening thud, junior football teammates David Page and 13-year-old Geoff Brock collided. It happened near the goals in a one-sided match as Geoff's team, Port Football Club's colts, was trying to score for the first time in their encounter against Risdon. Geoff reeled away from the collision, clutching his bloodied broken nose, his fractured little finger sticking out at an awkward angle.

Until this moment, Geoff had been standing the much bigger Gavin Herzich, one of the stars of the competition. The small blond-haired boy had been in and out of the team. Even though the wet conditions suited his low centre of gravity, his team was being beaten 30 goals to no score. But Herzich, Geoff's man, had not yet kicked a goal.

After the collision just before three-quarter time, Geoff was carried off the oval. Today, his eyes light up as he recounts how Herzich, no longer shadowed by his small but determined opponent, then kicked 12 goals in the last quarter.

'They considered me to be best-on-ground that day and I got four cans of Coke, a broken nose and broken pinky finger,' he laughed.

> *I played three or four more games and then I decided to forget it. It was too dangerous. One of my last matches was against*

Proprietary when Wayne Foster kicked 32 goals against us. Our team was coached by the great, late Max Goodwin and Bill Sayner and we were so small in stature that I was used as a ruckman a couple of times.

That was my 'fantastic' sport career. As a boy, my parents did not encourage me to play sport and could not afford for me to be involved. I used to go to Plenty Park to kick the ball with my mates Sammy Harris and John Power and other kids. We decided we would go and play football in the competition. I was doing a few odd jobs around the place, painting old wooden fences outside the trust homes for Mr Sayner, the trainer for Port Football Club juniors, and he asked me to come out to practice. I reckon he may have given me a pair of second-hand football boots.

In those days, more than 50 years ago, the other teams were Salesian College, Lutherans, Methodist, Risdon, Proprietary and Solomontown. We went out there with great intentions, but we were a small team and we had to face opponents such as Risdon and Salesian who had bigger guys.

Years later, after Mr Brock became the Independent Member for Frome, he was invited to be number-one ticket-holder for Port Football Club. He succeeded the previous Frome MP and Liberal Premier Rob Kerin. When attending his first event, a past players' and officials' dinner at the Port clubrooms, Geoff was amused to hear Rob Kerin introduce him with a chuckle as the man who took his spot in parliament and who took his position at the club.

As a boy, he used to make banners at home to take to the football so he could barrack for Port Football Club in style. His local heroes were Port's Tom Keain, formerly with Wandearah, and Port's drop-kicking expert and high-flier 'Daisy' O'Dea, as well as Spero Kotaras with Proprietary and the Valente boys and Mick Minervini at Solomontown.

'The Spencer Gulf League was so strong with teams from Port Pirie, Port Augusta and Whyalla. The league was unbeaten in inter-association matches for more than 20 years,' he said.

> *I would go to the football on Friday and Saturday nights and be in awe of the kicking and high marking. Magarey Medallist Jimmy Deane coached Port Football Club and had a milk round in the town. Bob Hammond also led Port and Risdon was coached by Dick Jackson. Port Adelaide coach Fos Williams came up for a match between his team and the SGL on Memorial Oval. Barrie Robran, who later won three Magarey Medals, came over with North Whyalla to play in Port Pirie.*
>
> *They would have been AFL superstars today. They played for peanuts and afterwards they would all gather for drinks. They were great days.*

Geoff Brock's blond-haired brother Peter played for the Port Football Club senior colts and used to be likened to Carl Ditterich of St Kilda. Another brother Keith also was a good footballer. Unsuccessful at football, Geoff tried cricket, thinking his talent in the backyard and at the beach would extend to the local pitches. He had to reconsider his options.

'I went out for a trial run, but the bowlers were so fast that I thought I would return to the backyard,' he said.

My football career was on a postage stamp, but I am a passionate Crows supporter and went to the very first match they played at Football Park. The hairs on my neck stood up and the adrenalin was pumping as we thrashed Hawthorn.

Unlike his interest in sport, his devotion to political heroes of the day was minimal. Politics was never discussed at the dinner table and he does not know to this day whether his parents favoured the Liberals or Labor.

'They were the only two major parties until Senator Don Chipp came in with the Australian Democrats in the 1970s,' he said.

I had no interest in politics until I went to Port Augusta to run the roadhouse. I was about 27 years old and started to watch the federal scene. In those days, the system was different with the national wage being determined in the Budget and people coming into the roadhouse to talk about the Liberals or Labor. I started to watch the vote counting on ABC television.

About the same time, the Dunstan Labor government in South Australia was looking at a proposed petro-chemical plant development at Redcliffs, south of Port Augusta. I discussed this with Ian McSporran of the Port Augusta City Council. When I returned to Port Pirie, I became involved in local government issues, dealing with then mayor, the late Bill Jones, who was one of my heroes.

Mr Jones worked as a public relations officer for the smelter, dabbled at ABC radio and the *Flinders News* while acting as the city's first citizen. He was famous for clashing with then Health Minister John Cornwall at the local shopping centre in a debate about lead contamination in Port Pirie.

'Everyone seemed to respect Mr Jones. He was a community person, showed leadership and portrayed himself with a feeling of confidence. I trusted him,' Geoff Brock said.

> *I would see him on occasion and chat to him. He would also be on the top table at the Smelter's Picnic lunches. I was there because I was assistant secretary of the BHAS Employees Picnic and Sports Association. I was later treasurer of the association for 15 years and had two stints as chairman. I was in awe of Mr Jones. No matter where you went, he was there.*
>
> *I also learned a lot from the late Denis Crisp who, as mayor, told me as a new councillor to sit there for 12 months and not say a word, just take it all in.*
>
> *I was taught that if you are going to say something, you need to make sure you have all your facts and figures or you can make yourself look silly. Without data, your comments are just another opinion.*

Geoff accepted an invitation to work as an official in the local electoral commission office during state and federal polls. He would help to tally the primary votes in elections and return home about 10.30 pm to watch the rest of the count on television.

'Arlene would say, 'Why are you watching that when you have been there all day?' he said.

> *I am a numbers man, that is why. The polling booth work was good pocket money because I was a labourer at the smelters at the time. And I saw the system first-hand and got to meet a lot of people again after losing contact with them when I was in the north.*

During this time, I was a polling booth assistant as well as returning officer on couple of occasions. The jobs lasted about 10 years in the 1980s and 1990s until I became mayor.

Later, the smelter's network of workers and their community club provided the opportunity for volunteer work. Geoff became involved in the BH Community Club through colleague Toby Wauchope, who suggested that he meet people and renew acquaintances after being away from Port Pirie and having just started work at the smelter.

'I picked up Toby from his mother's place and we went to the annual general meeting of the club. I came back as assistant secretary of the BHAS Employees Picnic and Sports Association,' Geoff Brock said.

The workers would gather in drinking 'schools' around the old horseshoe bar in the club on Friday nights. Geoff's group numbered 10 or 15 drinkers and included David Norton, Trevor Francis and Mike King. There was no light beer in those days and the drinks were all schooners, making for some memorable – or not so memorable – evenings.

The highlight on the club calendar was the Smelter's Picnic, an event that began more than a century before as an outing for smelter workers. It had developed into a holiday for the whole town with festivities including children's footraces, sideshows and a women's hen-chase at Crystal Brook. Working bees were conducted at the site during the year and Geoff Brock was among the volunteers.

'On picnic day, instead of travelling to Crystal Brook on the train with the kids waving water pistols, as we had done in the past, I drove there in my car,' he said.

In hindsight, my children missed out on those activities with me because I was always committed to helping with the operation of the picnic. I only saw Arlene and daughters Hayley and Marisa for about 15 minutes on the day. It is a regret.

I have tried very hard while I have been a minister to spend as much time as I can with my grandchildren in particular. Arlene missed out on a lot because I was on committees and serving as a councillor. She did a fantastic job raising our children.

I work in public office because I want future generations to have the best opportunities in a rapidly changing world.

The bond between Geoff Brock and his grandchildren is strong and the kids sometimes call into his electoral office and go to the front counter to see him. If Geoff is seeing a constituent, he will interrupt that meeting so he can take a few minutes for family time.

'In some cases, people lose all sense of reality about political figures, but we still have family out there. Sometimes family members need to speak to their dad or grandfather despite the fact they are in the public domain,' he said.

Politicians have always juggled family–work commitments at federal, state and local government levels, with some being more successful than others. Geoff was impressed by Liberal prime minister and treasurer, John Howard. 'When he became prime minister, I thought he had "grown" in stature,' he said. 'He believed in what he was doing. That is what attracted my admiration – the same as with our legendary former mayor, the late Bill Jones.'

Another Liberal treasurer, Peter Costello, was mostly in Mr Howard's shadow but formed a formidable tag-team with the leader.

Geoff Brock regarded him as a 'tremendous' performer. 'I followed the career of Labor leader Gough Whitlam and the "It's Time" campaign, which still resonates in my mind,' he said.

> *The Iraqi loans affair and the relationship between Labor's Jim Cairns and Junie Morosi contributed to Whitlam's downfall. It was not always plain sailing, but it was intriguing to watch. I thought Gough Whitlam was a great statesman and an impressive figure.*
>
> *There were some impressive partnerships in federal politics, for example Howard–Costello and Hawke–Keating. My dad always said Mr Hawke was fantastic and he solved many issues as president of the Australian Council of Trade Unions. He was a last-minute negotiator.*
>
> *In South Australia many years ago, Premier Tom Playford was a great leader. I wish I had the opportunity to see how he operated. I hear so many good stories about how Mr Playford would work with all sides to get an outcome for the betterment of SA. He started the Electricity Trust of SA and the automotive industry. He revolutionised this state.*
>
> *In the 1970s, I began to realise there were divisions within the major parties when Steele Hall broke away from the Liberal Party in South Australia to form the Liberal Movement. Later, when I was the BP Australia area manager based in Port Augusta, exploration companies wanted to develop the Roxby Downs uranium deposits in the outback. The Labor policy at the time was against uranium mining, but one of the party's MPs, 'Stormy Normy' Peterson, crossed the floor in parliament to allow the project to go ahead. He was expelled from the*

party. Without his crossing the floor and voting according to his conscience, we may not have had the Roxby Downs mine today.

I don't see that sort of thing happening in parliament today because we have stable government. If I was in a situation like 'Stormy Normy' was, then I would act, but I would hope it could be sorted out first within the parliament itself. I have crossed the floor quite a few times including about six occasions as a minister.

Geoff Brock in fact showed all the hallmarks of a maverick Independent when he responded to the first division, called in the House of Assembly after he was elected in 2014. Conflict between the major parties had been sparked by the actions of the Housing Trust Tenants Association regarding a possible 'bedroom tax' on public housing residents.

Liberal member for Morphett Duncan McFetridge moved that the House condemn the association for its 'despicable scare campaign and misleading and deceptive conduct in the 2014 election'. He said thousands of people had been distressed by the campaign and explained to parliament that the association was a small group with an assistant secretary who proclaimed herself to be a member of the Labor Party. Dr McFetridge quoted a peak housing body as saying the association had struck fear into the hearts of Housing SA tenants about losing their homes leading up to the election.

Incensed at the potential exploitation of vulnerable people via a letter circulated by the association, Geoff Brock crossed the floor to vote with the Opposition. He told the *Recorder* that he regretted forwarding the letter with a note warning residents they could be forced out of their homes or face the 'bedroom tax' under a Liberal government. Trust home tenants expressed fear, anger and distress at the thought of having to move out or pay a tax on spare bedrooms.

'I was verbally abused by several Labor MPs, but I exercised my vote as I saw fit,' Geoff Brock said of his actions in parliament. 'I think that is about the only time the government has lost a vote.' He had flexed his muscles, showing he was prepared to vote against the government on a principle.

Hardheaded political pundits say such behaviour enhances his value as a true Independent. It shows he is exercising his will to keep a government in power, but also holding it accountable. His critics say he should cross the floor more often. But on this occasion, in the new parliament after the 2014 poll, he adopted the role of a 'trailblazer' for independent spirit and is proud of his track record so soon after installing Jay Weatherill as premier.

In 2017, Geoff Brock repeated the dose by insisting that the government honour a condition of his kingmaker pact demanding accurate costing of political parties' election policies. Under the plan, adopted by parliament, a panel will verify costings and assess impacts on the state budget. The scheme intends to lend credibility to the political parties making the promises, but also to expose doubtful claims.

'Where does the money come from? That is what the panel will be asking,' Geoff said.

His timing could not have been better – less than 12 months remained until the next state election in March 2018. So much for the 'dithering, reluctant politician' . . . here was a politician making it difficult for his rivals to promote big-spending pledges to pull the carpet from beneath him. Geoff Brock had learned plenty from the cutthroat world in which he chose to mix.

Chapter 16

Independent

Questions linger about just how 'independent' Geoff Brock is, but he resolutely maintains this status. The indisputable fact is that he has never been a member of a political party. On the other hand, his support for the Rann and Weatherill Labor governments has been prominent. But he contends that he could have thrown his weight behind the Marshall Liberal team at the 2014 cliffhanger election had the conservatives been in a better position to claim minority government.

Can voters see Geoff Brock helping the Liberals into power? With both major parties staking strong claims to the outcome of the 2018 state election, it is not beyond the realm of possibility that Geoff could support the Liberals if they are in a position to form stable government. Again, it might depend on the deal that Geoff can extract from a would-be government to help his electorate.

He has an ability to court powerful identities on the state political stage. This flared into reality at the Blessing of the Fleet Ball at the Northern Festival Centre in Port Pirie in 2008. The ball, with its presentation of young debutantes, followed an afternoon ceremony when the statue of the Madonna was taken aboard a fishing boat on the Pirie River to enable the local Catholic bishop to bless the fishermen and their fleet.

Cr Dino Gadaleta, president of the Italian Community in Port

Pirie and a key supporter of Geoff Brock, was among the leading citizens at the ball, although he was taking a break from the president's role at the time. Cr Gadaleta chatted with special guest, state Attorney-General and Multicultural Affairs Minister Michael Atkinson, as the crowd enjoyed prawns and other seafood.

Later, as the revellers continued with their celebrations at the ball, Mr Atkinson spoke to Mr Brock. According to Michael Atkinson, Geoff Brock had said he was interested in running as a candidate for Frome for the Labor Party. Mr Atkinson reported that he had immediately responded: 'No, you will run as an Independent.'

As fate would have it, Geoff Brock did, indeed, run as an Independent to win the seat. When asked about their conversation, Michael Atkinson said he would leave it to others to speculate on his intentions in the conversation with Geoff, but agreed that it was wise advice.

'I don't think it would be appropriate for me to explain my thinking. It stands or falls on its own merits. I think people can make their own judgement,' he said.

Asked whether Geoff Brock had performed his role well as an Independent, Mr Atkinson, now Speaker of the House of Assembly, said: 'That is a matter for people in his electorate to judge rather than me, but obviously results of the election have placed him in an important position and he has acquitted himself well as a minister.'

Geoff Brock said Michael Atkinson may have suggested that he run as an Independent, but he had already decided to take that course of action. He then pointed to a meeting that took place before the Blessing of the Fleet Ball, at which he spoke to me, then in my role as managing-editor of the *Recorder*. Geoff said I was the first person, outside his inner circle, to be told of his plans to run as an Independent, and I can confirm this conversation took place.

'Mr Atkinson may have made those comments amid a lot of background noise at the ball,' Geoff said. 'If he did say I should run as an Independent, it was good advice, but I had already made up my mind.' He said there had been talk during the meeting about 'fast-tracking' future membership of the Labor Party for him.

Both major political parties had preselected candidates for 2010 and these had been brought forward to the 2009 by-election. I would not have taken the preselection from either side to the detriment of either candidate.

If I had run as the Labor candidate, I would not have been elected. I would never have wanted to be indebted to either side for whatever support they would have given me.

I owed my allegiance to my small band of dedicated supporters.

After Mr Brock told Mr Atkinson he was not interested in representing either party, the conversation turned to the fact that the by-election was three months away and there was a qualifying period for membership of the Labor Party.

'He broached the subject with me – no way in the world did I raise it,' Geoff said.

He indicated that if I wanted to become a member, they could fast-track it, but, in fact, I could have already been a member of a political party well and truly before that.

In the weeks before the ball, I was approached by both sides. I told the Liberal Party that I had not made a decision yet. Both sides said, 'Before you make a decision, come and see us.'

In 2014, Labor chose social worker and former shearer Marcus Connelly of Port Pirie to challenge for the seat. Mr Connelly sagely described it as having been a learning experience, insisting he had no grudges despite the party's inglorious support of his campaign. He finished third with 10 per cent of the vote in 2014, his preferences flowing to Geoff Brock.

Asked about his performance in his campaign, he replied: 'What campaign?'

The campaign was basically myself and union identity 'Nipper' Nitz. Limited support was given to me as a Labor candidate. Obviously the party supported Mr Brock and it turned out that was a good political move because it eventually gave them government. It was a complicated situation.

All parties put money where they are most likely to win seats and Frome didn't come into that category for Labor. So, consequently, they didn't support the candidate to any degree. That was a reasonable thing to do. But for a 'newbie' like me, it was difficult. If nothing else, I got to learn a lot more about the reality of politics.

Marcus Connelly had known that he was tackling a formidable opponent. He said Geoff Brock had a good relationship with Port Pirie and that people saw him as a leader.

Geoff was really great at maintaining that relationship. He was an excellent campaigner in the sense that he did it all the time. He was personable and made strong links with people. He helped people and they valued that. As an Independent, he played his cards right and he got extra benefits for Port Pirie.

I got heaps out of campaigning against Mr Brock even though it was a bit painful, difficult and sad at times when I didn't get the support.

I didn't hold anything against the Labor Party – it was how they had to play the game.

Marcus Connelly had no plans to recontest the seat at the time of his death in August 2017.

The Labor Party's ruthless approach, which he described and understood, resulted in Labor achieving government in 2014. Former South Australian Liberal senator, Sean Edwards, said Labor got across the line to form government because the Liberals, led by Steven Marshall, 'played by the rules' amid the drama of Geoff Brock's deliberations.

He said Mr Marshall had stayed away from Mr Brock when the Frome MP asked to be left alone with his family during the weekend after the poll.

'Geoff Brock is a nice fellow, but it is simply not enough to be that when you are a minister. Sadly, it seems enough for him to continue to win office in an electorate of 25,000 people or thereabouts by simply turning up to the opening of a chip packet,' Sean Edwards said.

The easiest card to play as an independent politician is to deliver government to the highest bidder in an election where there was a hung parliament. It is your moment in history to create a lasting legacy.

Mr Brock has failed to deliver beyond two things: the underwriting of the upgrade of the Nyrstar smelter in his home town and the gifting of a freshly minted ministry for the 'regions' for himself.

Since then, the scorecard on any objective assessment on innovative relevant economic or social policy in his portfolio is unremarkable. What characteristics make him likeable don't necessary make for a results-driven politician. It is not his fault. He was never that, but people elected him anyway.

Mr Brock has fallen into what many happy-go-lucky politicians have over history: he has confused movement with momentum. Incumbents who haven't done anything wrong are always hard to beat when up for re-election. They are resourced with offices and can effectively campaign every day while being paid to do the job anyway. Competing candidates have to give up their jobs and then turn up to everything Mr Brock attends and more while not being paid to do so.

Mr Edwards, who continues to be a businessman with interests in a Clare winery, said the Liberal state campaign had been 'solid' in 2014 with the party achieving 53.4 per cent of the popular vote. He said given that Mr Marshall was a relative newcomer with only 12 months in the leadership role, his performance was genuine and he was seen by most voters as the most credible candidate for premier on the day.

'The one thing the Liberal Party has done over many years is under-estimate the Labor Party's blood lust for power,' he said.

At the Liberal Party there is a tendency to play by Queensbury Rules. Mr Brock's plea for privacy on that all-so-important weekend following the 2014 election was respected by Mr

Marshall, but ignored by Mr Weatherill. It was another example of being out-flanked by a desperate caretaker premier who never expected to be even close in the contest.

Mr Weatherill's bursting into Mr Brock's home during the embargoed Brock-imposed reflection time, bearing pizza and a shiny new ministry was too much bling for Mr Brock, who was never a match for Weatherill's closing skills.

It was either coerce Brock or give way to the bright new Marshall plan for SA. Do or die. Mr Weatherill didn't hesitate to strike, leaving the Queensbury rules of boxing in tatters on the floor of the Liberal Party's campaign headquarters – again.

Chapter 17

'Getting My Hands Dirty'

Some of the major problems in the Frome electorate are solved over the front fence of a beautifully maintained garden in Port Pirie. On the rare weekends that Geoff Brock is at home, he can be found kneeling to tend the flowers and vegetables in the garden or mowing the lawn. Passers-by walking their dogs often stop to chat with the Independent Frome MP about matters of interest to them in the area. Motorists who spot the gardener at work will often do a U-turn and come back to park beside the footpath then get out of their car for a talk.

The house is immaculate with soaring trees and tidy flowerbeds. In fact, it features probably one of the best gardens in town, thanks to the work of Geoff and his partner Lyn. At Christmas, the couple join other residents in displaying twinkling festive lights at their property. They have hosted community picnics and Rotary Club of Port Pirie events in the outdoor surroundings.

'I love being in the garden getting my hands dirty,' Geoff Brock said. 'I became interested in gardening as a kid because Dad grew vegetables when we lived in Barry Street. I learned from him and loved doing it. In the early days, the vegetables were much needed by our family.'

Other leisure interests Geoff Brock enjoys include spending

time with his grandchildren and being involved with the Freemasons and the Rotary Club of Port Pirie.

He was approached to join the Freemasons' Lodge about the time of his election to parliament. He followed in the footsteps of his late father-in-law, Jack Cabrie. Mr Cabrie would wear his Freemasons' regalia at the family home before attending Lodge meetings, but never talked about the secret practices of the fellowship.

'It was a great privilege to be asked to join because of him. Because of time constraints, I have not been able to attend a Lodge meeting for many years, but I have maintained contact and made many friends across South Australia among the brethren, including other politicians,' he said. 'The Lodge supports other organisations across Australia and SA. They do a lot behind the scenes for groups and associations and they have become more open about their activities. You see Lodge members running barbecues and other events.'

With a smile, he added: 'The Freemasons have a certain greeting – you can tell when someone is a member by their handshake. I have met other members during my parliamentary career.'

Not bound by such rules of confidentiality, Rotary has been more relaxed, but is still a mutually beneficial pursuit for Geoff who, in 2009, was asked to be president of the local club for 2010–11. By this time, he had been elected to represent Frome in parliament.

The Rotary meetings were on Thursday night so Geoff Brock had to travel back from parliament during sitting sessions to chair the club meetings at the local golf club.

'It was a great honour to be president. Whenever a political drama or event came up in the media, the club's sergeant-at-arms would fine me 50 cents for my involvement in politics. It was a lot of fun and I still attend when I can,' he said.

Rotary's main focus is the worldwide fight against polio. Our club's projects included providing aid to the Philippines. Our members have done great things over there, supplying fresh water to some of the outlying areas and sending equipment to schools.

We have sent our shelterboxes, which provide emergency tents, cooking utensils and sleeping gear. Old medical and dental equipment and schoolbooks have been forwarded to the islands.

As president, I visited our sister club Dau on a trip I funded myself. I had to make it clear I was not there as an MP otherwise there would have been a security contingent. They are very protective of their politicians over there.

Also making the trip with the Port Pirie delegation was Rotarian Cr Dino Gadaleta, a staunch member of Geoff Brock's election campaign team. Cr Gadaleta had packed souvenirs from Port Pirie – six electioneering 'Vote Brock' T-shirts that the locals decided to wear during an official barbecue at the Dau president's house.

'By displaying them, the locals honoured me,' Geoff Brock said.

In the outlying areas, the contingent trekked along goat tracks with Filipino guides to mountain villages where the people shared their meagre food with them. 'It showed us how lucky we are, although they were happy and wanted to share everything with us,' he said.

Geoff was also mindful during his presidency of the needs of Port Pirie residents. His club raised $30,000 for shade sails over the playground at Flinders View Park near the Port Pirie foreshore. This was Geoff Brock's President's Project.

'I have been privileged to be involved with Rotary and the Freemasons, two organisations that have their own ways of operating and have their own mythologies,' he said.

Helping others less fortunate than himself is a theme that runs through Geoff's life. In 2012, he attended a Camp Quality event at Wallaroo and was amazed at the spirit of children with terminal illnesses. As part of the event, supporters travelled to the Cornwall Hotel in Moonta, run by Geoff's step-daughter Jackie Aldridge and her husband Scott. When Geoff was invited to make a speech, he was overwhelmed by the moment.

'The words would not come out, no matter how hard I tried. I remember it vividly. I just had to walk away and someone else took over,' he said.

But Geoff Brock is not lost for words when the topics of electricity and water come up in the conversation. He looks back on late Liberal premier Tom Playford's era when the legendary figure set up the electricity network in city and country areas as the Electricity Trust of South Australia.

'It was far-sighted to have the state running the electricity network. This was similar to the concepts of the South Australian Railways and the Commonwealth Railways,' he said.

> *A lot of governments across Australia have sold assets, but once we get into privatisation, we have shareholders who have to be*

satisfied with their returns and the governments lose control of vital services such as power, rail and water.

Hindsight is a wonderful thing, but we need to ensure the same thing doesn't happen with health and education. If schools were privatised, how would that affect people who are less financially well off? We need to look at the big picture.

Geoff Brock wonders whether the 'big picture' should also include better use of the nation's resources of oil, gas and uranium. 'We don't seem to be able to benefit from them,' he said.

For about five years, he has championed a $6 billion plan to pipe water from the Ord River across the top of Australia then down through the Red Centre to the Murray–Darling Basin to boost supplies in that system. The feasibility study alone for the project would cost $500,000, but the extra 6000 gigalitres that would become available (a fraction of the huge quantity of water that actually flows into the ocean from the Ord River) would dramatically transform farms and towns.

The pipeline would follow the Adelaide–Darwin railway through the heart of Australia with gas-powered pumping stations dotting the route and diversions set up for irrigation to cattle stations along the way. Geoff Brock said he had spoken to resources company Chevron, which was interested in the project.

Geoff shared a common interest in major water projects with Queensland-based federal MP Bob Katter, who he met in Canberra to discuss the plan. The idea was also floated with then Western Australian premier Colin Barnett and the then leader of the Nationals in WA.

'It could be another Snowy Mountains Hydro Scheme, only it would be a pipeline through the desert. It would be a nation-building scheme,' Mr Brock said. 'It would fulfil the dreams of former Western Australian Water Minister Ernie Bridges. I would pursue the idea as a local parliamentarian, not as a minister, because it would be good for Port Pirie, located at the end of the Murray–Darling water system.'

Reflecting the views of the people of the state, Geoff Brock is undecided on the merits of nuclear power despite noting that Australia has some of the world's biggest uranium deposits. He advocates public discussion on the topic, particularly so that safeguards can be explored. Referring to the Liberals stance on the nuclear power option, he said there was no bipartisan support for debate 'so that discussion has ceased'.

'Some say nuclear power may not be economically viable, sustainable or safe, but if we don't talk about all these issues, how do we know?' he said.

Suggesting there may be local interest in nuclear-waste storage or power generation, he said the mayors of the Spencer Gulf cities had looked at the operation of the Lucas Heights nuclear-medicine reactor in Sydney.

'If we go nuclear, it could generate power for all of Australia,' he said.

Economic development has been pursued relentlessly by Geoff Brock. This now includes about $850 million in projects in Port Pirie including the smelter transformation, the city-centre upgrade, dredging and boat ramp development, the sport hub (which received $5 million negotiated by Geoff in his balance-of-power deal) and a retail project worth up to $80 million.

The retail project includes an ALDI supermarket on a site located in Wandearah Road, halfway between the city centre and the Pirie Plaza shopping centre. Special dispensation was needed from the government – and sought by Geoff Brock – for the project to go ahead partly on land sub-leased from the Port Pirie Harness Racing Club.

The original *Port Pirie Racecourse Act* of 1949 had meant that the club could only sub-lease its land for sport activities, but this was changed to allow many thousands of dollars in yearly lease fees to flow to the club from the retail tenants, a non-sport organisation.

Geoff Brock said former Labor upper house president Ron Roberts, of Port Pirie, had tried to bring about changes to the Act for 20 years before the breakthrough. Without the change, the land could simply have been sold to the developers by the Crown, denying the harness racing club a dividend. The project is the first step towards a chain of shops from the city centre to the Pirie Plaza. If it can be achieved, it would be the biggest commercial retail precinct in country South Australia.

Crucial to Port Pirie's future is clean air. The town's lead smelter has operated for more than 125 years. There is now the promise of dramatic reductions in lead-in-air under the transformation.

'I know Port Pirie people are proud of what the smelter has done,' Geoff Brock said.

> *I have seen vast improvements in emissions over many, many years to where we are today, a great project that will basically eliminate all emissions from the plant.*
>
> *This community and the smelter have been world leaders in recognising the concern for our children's health. We have dealt*

> *with that as a community and work together to achieve great results with community lead-abatement programs. Other lead facilities from across the world have come to Port Pirie to see how we handle it.*
>
> *Despite the concerns, we have had some highly successful residents; great people who have lived here and travelled elsewhere, achieving wonderful international careers.*

While he is up-to-the-minute with his developmental aspirations for Port Pirie and South Australia, Geoff Brock is not quite so progressive with the social issue of gay marriage.

'I think it is a union of a couple and I respect that, but using the word "marriage" is a bit different,' he said. 'In South Australia, there is legislation to recognise the union of same-sex couples,' he said. He added that he has friends who are gay. 'Everyone is different,' he said.

On another topic that makes headlines, Geoff said the rise of United States President Donald Trump showed voters were disillusioned with mainstream politics; they were questioning the Establishment. 'Protest votes are happening around the world,' he said.

> *We need to work with whoever is elected in various countries. I will work with those people. In Australia, we have the rise of Nick Xenophon, more recently the ascent of veteran Bob Katter and emergence of Pauline Hanson. I would like to see everyone sit around the table and come to a compromise.*
>
> *We have to change, but not to the detriment of low-income earners. The federal government wants to save costs, but it keeps hitting people who can afford it the least.*

Politics sometimes gets in the way of progress. I would like the government and opposition to acknowledge the positions of the other side. We are all working for the one thing, why do we have these divisions? Political parties are not united in themselves behind the scenes. I am lucky that my voice is heard in state Cabinet and I feel comfortable being part of the ministry.

Chapter 18

Deeds or Words?

Is a statesman measured by deeds or words? In the case of Geoff Brock, oratorical skills rank second to his achievements. He is not a 'silver-tongue', but therein lies the attraction. His mashing of the language is legendary. He refers to 'that thing there' and 'that stuff' while arguing a point or outlining a project for the community. But, when he is in full flight and speaking from the heart, he is gritty and compelling.

In the interviews for this book, Geoff Brock has at times taken indecisive approaches to various subjects, but at other moments, particularly when talking about his childhood, he is evocative, earthy and direct.

With tears streaming down his cheeks, he told of the fateful day his wife was taken from him in a road smash. On another occasion, he was matter-of-fact in describing how his late mother had sold household furniture to raise money with which to buy food for the family during his childhood in Port Pirie.

Geoff Brock has what many politicians, sport heroes and bosses would love to have – the common touch. His parents were working class, but he moved into the middle class with white-collar jobs before entering the political arena. That arcane world is filled with people from the 'machines' of both left and right politics, career opportunists who jump at the first chance to run for parliamentary office. Many have university degrees, in such disciplines as arts and law, and others have high-profile business backgrounds. They indulge in 'pollie speak', worry about focus groups and rely heavily on advisers.

Geoff Brock is refreshingly simple in his approach. 'I have come in as a normal "Joe Blow"; someone who has done community work before being elected. I have not been tainted by in-grown, preconceived ideas about politics,' he said.

> *I do get criticised because I am not as eloquent as a lot of politicians but I don't apologise for that. I don't want to be something that I am not. I am not the most polished speaker, but I speak from my heart. I have been told I should be less emotional. I get affected by things out there and that comes through in my speeches. I am not a silver-tongue, but if I get criticised for that, so be it.*

On the federal scene, politicians have been described as 'authentic' and this is an apt description for the Member for Frome, who fits easily into an unpretentious town. His love for the 'best large community in South Australia' has been repaid by the citizens of Port Pirie with his resounding success at the ballot box.

'The thing that I like about Port Pirie is that it is a close and caring community despite having many knocks over the years,' Geoff said.

> *We have lost businesses and government enterprises such as the railways and we have been promised many things, but we bounce back. It is now 40 years since I returned to Port Pirie after a few years in Port Augusta running a roadhouse,*

which was a dream-come-true despite my parents' opposition to the idea.

My community has always been there for me through my personal challenges and tragedies. We did lose belief in ourselves after all the knocks Port Pirie received over many years. But we have started to believe in ourselves again and I see that flowing from the smelters transformation.

Port Pirie people are down-to-earth and I am no different, just a very average person. I have been fortunate to have had opportunities and I believe that if a door opens, you put your foot inside and see where it leads.

Newcomers to the town fall in love with the people and way of life, although it takes time. Some years ago, new business people in town confided to Geoff that they deliberately arrived with their wives and families at night, believing darkness would hide the grim, industrial entrance to the town and ease the impact of relocation.

'People say that you cry when you first see Port Pirie and you cry when you leave,' Geoff Brock said.

We hear stories about people transferring here for work and planning to stay for only a short time. But when they leave, they do so reluctantly and have great memories of their time here.

Some of our residents have hit the big time overseas and still have great affection for the town. And we have produced some great sportspeople in swimming, tennis, hockey, cricket, football, baseball and gymnastics.

We now have the best opportunities that we have ever had in our history and we need to grab them and not let go.

Geoff Brock has only one regret about his life in Port Pirie – not driving his wife Arlene to Warnertown on the day that she later died in a car crash. He was unable to take her on the journey because he needed to be at work at the smelter for a meeting with unions.

Local connections are never far away when Geoff Brock is talking to the government hierarchy in Adelaide. He considers himself a 'piece of Port Pirie' when he comes to the offices of the premier and treasurer in his regular meetings with the leaders. For up to 45 minutes every week, he chats with Premier Jay Weatherill in the State Administration Centre.

Relishing these moments, Geoff gazes over Mr Weatherill's shoulder at the high-rise view stretching out towards Victoria Square while championing local causes.

'We talk about everything including what is happening in the regions around the state, what is happening in Frome, and other subjects relating to my portfolios,' he said.

> *We have been through the 57 concessions that were granted to me as Independent Member for Frome. There are only three remaining concessions to be fulfilled and that will happen soon.*
>
> *I also meet Treasurer Tom Koutsantonis every week. He is always welcoming and showed his support by providing almost $7 million extra for the Regional Development Fund. We talk about opportunities for the state. If I have an issue, it is an ideal opportunity for me to talk to the top men.*

His access to the leaders has sparked comments from some Labor MPs that he has better access than they do.

At the start of every parliamentary session, Geoff Brock is briefed on the order of business and legislation for debate by government whip Tom Kenyon.

With powerful contacts in government, Geoff is able to achieve most of his desired outcomes through behind-the-scenes negotiations.

'I have my say in Cabinet and question lots of things, but most of my work is done in the background,' he said.

Despite the financial largesse, Geoff Brock is rated much higher 'as an individual' than as a politician, at least according to Ceduna mayor, Allan Suter.

The coastal township on the Eyre Peninsula is not without its social and economic problems, but Mr Suter is buoyed by the minister.

'Geoff Brock was highly supportive of our area when it came to getting funding for a fish unloading facility that we had been chasing for 10 years,' he said. 'Without Mr Brock, we would not have gained government funding support. I could not rate him more highly – he is honest and supportive.'

But Mr Suter added a qualification to his strong sentiments. 'I think Mr Brock signed his own death warrant when he went with the present government, which doesn't reflect well on anyone,' he said.

On the other side of the state, Mount Gambier mayor Andrew Lee strongly supports Geoff Brock. Mr Lee migrated from Hong Kong in 1990, but had trouble finding a job until he moved to Mount Gambier where he opened the Mandarin Restaurant. He was happy to welcome Geoff Brock as Regional Development Minister: 'Without him, I don't think we could have this sort of attention from the government.'

With Geoff Brock's 'hard work and pushing', he said, councils around the state received a couple of million dollars to provide youth traineeships. 'Mr Brock is easy-going. I like him. I ring him and sometimes he calls me back regarding one or two issues. He is a decent gentleman,' he said.

And taking the pro-Brock spotlight back to the centre of the state, the Mid North, there is praise from the Golden North ice cream factory. The company's managing director, Peter Adamo, said Mr Brock had been an excellent advocate and supporter for South Australian regional businesses.

'Mr Brock understands our predicament of being based in a rural town and competing on a national level,' he said.

> *He has shown a genuine interest in the growth and sustainability of Golden North and visits our factory on a yearly basis to see our growth and development. He and his team's commitment to the region has seen capacity building of regional community, creating sustainable economic benefit to the region and state.*

Despite the praise, one does not have to venture far into the population to find adverse reactions to the man who proclaims he has a conscience.

One commentator said Geoff Brock was 'a puppet for the Labor government' and was 'being used in a game' of propping up a mirage of regional development initiatives.

'The truth is he cannot see it,' the observer said. 'He genuinely means well and wants to help people, but the government knows there are no votes in the country for Labor. Mr Brock has done nothing for country South Australia that he could not have done if he had gone to the other side of politics.'

This assertion flies in the face of the numbers – the Liberals would have lacked enough seats to form government in 2014 even if Geoff Brock had thrown his weight behind them. It is academic what would have happened if he had 'gone to the other side'.

At a 2017 Community Forum attended by ministers at a Clare Town Hall filled almost to capacity, Premier Jay Weatherill said Mr Brock 'reminded us' frequently in Cabinet that he was an Independent. During the same round of Mid North visits, the Country Cabinet attracted an unprecedented crowd to the bowling club at Balaklava.

At the Port Pirie forum on the Country Cabinet circuit members of Geoff Brock's Rotary Club cooked the barbecue for the visiting ministers, their entourage and residents. In welcoming the crowd and outlining the program, Premier Mr Weatherill singled out Geoff for 'special mention'.

'Thank you for once again bringing us to your beautiful part of the world,' he said.

> *Geoff not only makes a massive contribution to Cabinet, but has been a champion for the regions around South Australia, no more so than for his beloved seat of Frome, and particularly the city of Port Pirie. I don't think there has been a more fierce advocate for the upgrade of the smelter. A few short years ago, the plant was facing closure due to lead pollution.*
>
> *Port Pirie was the ugly duckling of the Nyrstar global network. It is now, with a new multi-metal processing facility, at the centre of their global economic operations. That is an extraordinary transformation. It gives the region the opportunity to retell the story of itself. You only have to gaze*

at the Flinders Ranges to understand this is one of the most beautiful places in our nation.

Rather than a story of town with lead pollution and a town in decline, it should be the story of a town with an incredibly bright future. Thanks, Geoff, for all you have done to allow this town to retell the story of itself.

Chapter 19

Mentors

'Bob Such taught me to navigate the unknown.'

With these words Frome Independent MP Geoff Brock described how Dr Such, a maverick former Liberal minister turned Independent, was a great mentor to him. Dr Such was elected as a Liberal in 1989 to the seat of Fisher, was a minister in the Brown Liberal government, served as speaker and became an Independent in 2002.

A week after being re-elected in 2014, Dr Such was diagnosed with a brain tumour. At the time, he and Mr Brock held the key to the outcome of the poll. The genial doctor died later that year.

'Bob was a fantastic adviser with a good understanding of the role of Independents,' Geoff Brock said. 'He had been a great supporter in those first few days after the 2014 poll and I missed him once he withdrew from the political scene for health reasons. He was a great man.'

Another of Geoff Brock's confidants was then Independent Kris Hanna. A former Labor and Greens parliamentarian, Mr Hanna was defeated in the seat of Mitchell in 2014 and later became mayor of Marion. Over coffee in Parliament House, Mr Hanna and Dr Such played pivotal, friendly roles for the fledgling Independent Mr Brock in the first year after he was elected in 2009.

'Without those guys, I would have struggled,' he said. 'If anyone from the major parties advised me, they would have been leaning to their causes.

> *Dr Such would say after question time that he was 'doing no good here' and would return to his electorate office where he could achieve greater things.*
>
> *I could not return to my electorate office 250 kilometres away and so I stayed in parliament where I kept up with paperwork and debates. I had plenty of time to reflect on where I stood in the scheme of things.*
>
> *Until Dr Such's leave of absence because of sickness, he guided me through some of my toughest challenges. I will be forever grateful to him.*

To some extent, there is silence from the Opposition in response to Geoff Brock's interest in the deliberations of the House of Assembly. He was told in 2014 when he became a minister that he would be offered briefings from the Opposition on legislative Bills introduced to the House, but this never happened.

'When the Opposition introduces Bills, they don't offer a briefing on their proposals. The first that I hear about it is when the Bills hit parliament. I think it is wrong. I have to make a decision on what I see then and there. Sometimes I have asked for a briefing,' he said. 'When the government wants to introduce legislation, I receive a briefing in Cabinet.'

Despite now being considered as a veteran of the parliament, Geoff is still learning.

'I watch how others operate and how ministers operate especially, but they don't give me one-on-one meetings or anything like that. I suppose I learn more through talking to people outside the House. Some days I will have five or six people call at my parliamentary office,' he said.

The views of the people ultimately guided him when he was considering euthanasia laws.

When a conscience vote sponsored by Independent Bob Such failed in the parliament in 2012, Geoff Brock had been among those voices opposing the introduction of mercy killings. He now says he took that stance out of ignorance because he had failed to consult residents on what they wanted him to do.

In late 2016, the issue resurfaced with Port Pirie cancer patient Kylie Monaghan leading a nationally publicised campaign for euthanasia laws. This time, Geoff listened to his community and voted in favour of the change. Despite his support, the Bill was defeated on the casting vote of Speaker Michael Atkinson.

Geoff Brock calls it the 'Death with Dignity' vote and says the vast majority of people in Frome supported the proposed new laws in six surveys that he conducted. Residents also called at his house in Port Pirie to express their views. The debate on the legislation continued until 4.30 am on 17 November 2016 in the House of Assembly with many amendments being proposed and speakers for and against.

'I was encouraged by both sides of the debate not to take part in the final vote,' Geoff Brock said.

> *Some said it was a 'touchy subject' and I did not have to vote. Others said that I looked tired and perhaps I should go home to my unit in Adelaide. I felt strongly that I should stick around and that I had a democratic duty to cast my vote.*

In the days leading to the verdict, he spoke to euthanasia advocate and television personality Andrew Denton, but was unable to contact Kylie Monaghan because she was too sick. Kylie died in Port Pirie hospital the day before a *60 Minutes* interview about her campaign was screened on Channel 9. It was unlikely that another bid for the change would be sought in the term of this parliament.

Many, like Geoff Brock, think the issue should be determined by the federal government to give uniformity of laws around the nation.

'That would reflect just how big an issue this is,' he said.

> *I was feeling pretty emotional about the whole thing. Coming up through the ranks, I did not have a hardened skin. If I was going to be a career politician, I would have started at 25 years old, not 59. It is hard when you are judged by people who have never spoken to you, but I voted in the way my community wanted me to.*

Residents, political opponents and other observers had been holding their breath, waiting for a decision about whether Geoff Brock would run for office again in 2018. He confirms he will recontest his seat, but is not looking too far into the future.

'I will campaign at the next election, God-willing that I have good health. Life can change on a whim. I will just do it one year at a time,' he said.

> *If I am re-elected, I will be very grateful and will do the best I can. We will see what happens. What will Port Pirie, our regions and our state be like in 10 years' time? It is no good thinking just about the near future.*

I have ideas about the water pipeline from the north of Australia to the southern states and have proposed a high-temperature furnace for Port Pirie to treat waste. People on both sides say to me that I think too far down the track and that I may not be here to see the benefits. Some councils and governments have a vision only for their term of office. We need a long-term vision of where our country is going to be in 20 years' time.

Chapter 20

Yin and Yang

While in the local, state and national spotlight, Geoff Brock has juggled a successful private life. He keeps close contact with his family members. He and partner Lyn begin every year by opening their calendar to their 14 grandchildren. School excursions, birthdays, plays, netball grand finals and football presentations and myriad other special moments are listed in their diary after talking to the family members. Geoff or Lyn or both of them manage to attend every event. They find unity in their love of their children and grandchildren and their common belief in the importance of his work.

There is a healthy dose of yin and yang in the relationship between Geoff Brock and his partner Lyn Akker. While Geoff is away travelling the state as a minister or immersed in paperwork in their sprawling house, Lyn, in the best traditions of the ancient Chinese concept, may be fixing a doorknob or shovelling crusher dust. In Oriental philosophy, yin and yang represent the principle that all things exist as opposites, but when in correct balance, they produce harmony.

Lyn, a hairdresser for 40 years, met Geoff Brock in 1993, bringing with her a strong practical streak that was fostered by her late father Trevor Richardson when her family lived in Kapunda and Burra.

'My dad used to take me out to the shed and show me how to do most things, whether it was fixing a washing machine or shovelling dirt. I used to resent it, but I now realise it has shaped my character,' she said.

Recently, I shovelled about 20 metres of crusher dust to make an outdoor area at our home. Geoff is rarely at home so I am the shoveller and fixer. People don't expect that. They come here and I will be fixing a doorknob, putting something together or working outside.

Lyn is an astute judge of character and has proved a great foil for Geoff in assessing personalities on the political scene.

'We started from the bottom, step by step,' Lyn says while sitting in a white wicker chair in her hairdressing salon at the rear of their home.

I was shy when mixing with people while accompanying Geoff. I had been accustomed to chatting to people as a hairdresser, but this was a new role. Geoff wears his heart on his sleeve and is probably too open as a person.

I have been humbled by the support that we have had along the way. The premier has been very good to Geoff, as has the treasurer. And he could never have done what he has without the support of his staff both here and in Adelaide. They do the grinding, groundbreaking work such as organising the Country Cabinet visit to Frome in 2017. We owe thanks to their loyalty and hard work.

Lyn could relate to the shock experienced by the Brock family when Arlene died because she and her sister and brother lost their father suddenly when she was 21 years old.

'The blows received in life give you character. What doesn't kill you makes you stronger,' she said.

I respect Geoff's commitment to his family and his job, but he tries to be all things to all people and spreads himself too thinly. It has been his long-standing dream to be able to help Port Pirie and the region. He thinks the sun shines brighter and the grass grows greener in Port Pirie.

But it has been a very steep learning curve for me. It has changed us and we have all had to step up. I have had to push myself and face my fears because I am a homebody and family person and I never thought we would be in the public eye. There are things that I could have done better, but I have given it my best shot.

Lyn related a story of an official dinner they attended early in Geoff's political career:

I always look at the bright side and think of the funny things that have happened. At one of the first dinners we attended, the speeches went on and on. Finally, the chicken meal arrived, but it was rather hard and as I put my fork in it it flicked onto a politician's lap beside me. He enjoyed spinning that story for a very long time.

One of Lyn's strongest memories is of an encounter with a woman at the World Cup cricket game between Pakistan and India at Adelaide Oval in 2015. The small Vietnamese woman struck up a conversation and said Mr Brock visited her house regularly, much to Lyn's astonishment.

It turned out that the woman was the wife of Governor Hieu Van Le and the house frequented by Geoff was Government House. It was part of his official duties to attend there and sign papers.

'Mr and Mrs Le have such an intense story. They came by boat from Vietnam and they nearly died on the trip,' she said.

Lyn sees her role in the partnership with Geoff as 'keeping the home fires burning' and looking after the kids and caring for him at low moments such as sickness. She allocates up to five shirts and ties each week for the minister to take to Adelaide with him during parliamentary sittings.

With Geoff always pushing himself to his limits, she was heartened when he was allocated a ministerial car and driver.

'I used to think the arrangement was a total luxury and unnecessary expense for the government, but with all the travel that Geoff does, it gives me peace of mind that he is being driven on his journeys,' she said.

Chapter 21

2018 Referendum

After hours of interviews and research regarding the climb to power of the Independent Member for Frome, it came down to a heartfelt revelation: he doubts himself.

We were sitting in the rosewood interior of Geoff Brock's electorate headquarters on a Sunday morning. Just a few doors down, the local credit union office was undergoing a major interior refit – an example of the resurgence of the economy in Port Pirie.

The Cabinet minister was talking about possible scenarios as he seeks, in 2018, to win his fourth election as the member. Stating the obvious, he said he was uncertain whether the voters would re-elect him. The conversation soon led back to the events of 2014 when he handed power to the Weatherill Labor government using his balance-of-power vote.

Geoff Brock said the 2018 election would be a 'referendum' on whether he had done the right thing as a kingmaker. He spoke of a possible revolving door of government if he had failed to act to assure stable administration back then. 'My first concern was for Port Pirie,' he said.

'Have I done the right thing by the people, by South Australia and by the regions? I will be judged on what has been done and the extra focus on the regions. I see it as a 'review' of what happened in 2014. I hope they see the truth and the agony I had to go through.'

Some people, mostly non-Labor voters, have vowed to never speak to Geoff Brock again as a result of his manoeuvre to support Mr Weatherill. They criticised him in emails and on social media.

Yet there is support from some businesses sympathetic to Labor. Geoff has advocated for them in his role as a parliamentarian. 'They still communicate with me,' he said.

Indeed, many businesses share his goal of transforming country SA. Two 'corridors' of enterprise are the centrepiece of his latest activities and have involved much communication with business and industry. One 'corridor' is the area from Two Wells to Whyalla, which has $4 billion allocated to projects. It includes market gardening and agriculture, industry, renewable energy, abattoirs and meat processing. It is boosted by water development, aviation, gas, power, ports and environmental features. He launched the prospectus for opportunities in this area with the promise of 'untold potential for development'.

The other swathe of economic activity is from Mount Barker to Bordertown, including Murray Bridge, with a similar value of projects. These include industries involving almonds, poultry and agriculture, potential for aviation training at Renmark and development of motor sport at Tailem Bend.

'In both these corridors, I have been trying to get the government to look more towards regional SA,' he said.

Geoff Brock is leaving giant footprints across the state. Following the demise of his Port Augusta roadhouse business in 1977, Geoff has dedicated the rest of his life to Port Pirie, the town of his birth, with the community, in turn, embracing him and his family.

'People will look back and see that at least this person had a shot at it,' he said. 'The community has given me an opportunity that I never thought I would have achieved when I was at school, not in my wildest dreams, and I just want to give back as much as I can for the people.'

And what of the future for this region? The year 2016 was not a good one for the Upper Spencer Gulf. The Arrium steelworks at Whyalla was put into administration with billions of dollars in debts and the environmentally challenged, coal-fired Northern Power Station closed at Port Augusta, throwing hundreds of people out of work.

But 2017 saw the government heading in the right direction as the gulf zone was 'born again'. The steelworks was sold to a United Kingdom company with a reputation for rebuilding stricken assets. Whyalla was out of the doldrums and recovering.

And Carriewerloo Station near Port Augusta was named as the location for a $650 million solar-thermal power plant – the world's biggest – to be built by a United States firm to offer cheaper power for the masses. An incredible 650 jobs were to be created during construction and 50 positions would be needed to operate the plant. Port Augusta, too, had hit its straps and was back in the game.

Geoff Brock had linked his fortunes to the Repower Port Augusta group in the northern city since his election in 2009, attending meetings at which these locals campaigned for the solar-thermal project.

'The Upper Spencer Gulf has certainly changed from what it was 12 months ago,' he said.

To outline the new venture, Premier Weatherill, Treasurer Tom Koutsantonis and Mr Brock met cheering residents at the Port Augusta recreation centre on 15 August 2017.

'The crowd was absolutely ecstatic,' he said.

> *Port Pirie's smelter is scheduled to open its $660 million redevelopment in 2018 and Whyalla is back on track. Years ago the gulf region was a powerhouse of the old technology. The cities have transformed to become a powerhouse again for the South Australian economy with new technology and innovation.*
>
> *Nyrstar will pioneer an e-waste treatment operation while the steelworks will have state-of-the-art steel-making technology with power co-generation. Port Augusta's solar-thermal project will offer innovative renewable technology.*

But does this new cycle of investment and potential prosperity suggest that something was amiss in the preceding era? A prominent figure familiar with regional economics and development puts it bluntly: 'By coming full circle, it suggests policy failure in the intervening years.'

He suggested there had been a lack of investment in the gulf region and the Eyre Peninsula and that other areas bordered on 'third-world conditions' with a period of 'darkness' economically.

'You have to look at the overall dispersal of capital and where productivity lays,' he said.

> *This government started in 2002 off the back of policies that were about building primary industries and food and wine . . . it has been a failure between then and now with wasted opportunities. Streaky Bay has had 14 blackouts since the big power failure in September 2016. What is being done about it?*

> *Before Mr Brock arrived on the scene, we didn't have a lot to compare him with. He is a lovely bloke and he has tried hard, but he is working with consummate politicians.*
>
> *I would give him full points for trying, but the guys he is swimming with are professional politicians. I don't think Mr Brock is a professional politician and that is a good thing*

The source said that Geoff Brock had shone in regional development, but his performance as Local Government Minister had been underwhelming.

'I don't get a great sense of optimism,' the commentator said.

> *The government and Mr Brock as minister have failed in their responsibilities in regard to local governance, which is the closest form of government to the people. There are crises all over the place. It is swept under the rug to a large degree, but the more you do that, the bigger the problem becomes.*

Another commentator, this time from academia, did not see any substantial reforms in the administration's responsibility for local government in the past four years. He said regional development, from both an economic and social perspective, had no 'substantive framework' so that 'activity is simply that, activity'.

> *Funding of individual companies on an application-based system is not economic development; it is not even industry development nor regional or town and city economic development. It is simply funding companies on an application-based process with no cost-benefit analysis undertaken at all. One must ask why investment proposals are not undertaken*

by the companies concerned if they are seeking to develop their business.

An impartial observer would have to ask what have we achieved in economic and social development of any consequence in the past four years.

Another identity with extensive high-level local government experience agreed the council sector was in crisis and needed reform with an emphasis on efficiency.

Geoff Brock responded by saying he had led changes to the *Local Government Act* to provide more clarity in an era of inquiries by both the ombudsman and Independent Commission Against Corruption. The responsibility for overseeing boundary changes and merged responsibilities has been taken from the Boundary Facilitation Adjustment Commission and handed to the Local Government Grants Commission. This is considered to be a simpler process and Geoff Brock said the commission would 'know each council' through its distribution of federal funds.

'It has been a long and tedious process to overhaul the procedures – sending drafts to parliamentary counsel and sometimes Crown Law, seeking consultation with communities and the Local Government Association and then debate in both Houses of parliament,' he said.

It is all coming together and a group of about six councils on the Eyre Peninsula will be in a pilot program to look at streamlining activities and working more efficiently with neighbouring councils. I have been able to provide the foundations for whoever is in government or whoever is the minister, after the 2018 election, to move more freely with discussions with relevant councils. The hard decisions have to be made in the new government.

I have stressed to councils that they need to look at their population bases regarding duplication – can they share resources with other councils? Could these shared resources be machinery, information technology, payroll and planning officers and chief executive officers? There are many councils now sharing their resources and it doesn't need to be with an adjoining municipality.

If I am Local Government Minister again, I would be looking in some cases at having one chief executive officer for more than one council. Instead of paying $250,000 yearly for a small council to have a chief executive officer, with the salary coming from a small municipal rate base, you would have that officer covering more than one council. The hospital system has already done this with their structure. As a result of sharing chief executive officers, more money would be released for capital works.

Meanwhile, in some circles, Geoff Brock is thought to have 'woken up' the government to regionalisation with Port Pirie being a 'winner'.

Chapter 22

Keeping His Head

Is Geoff Brock an ordinary man in extraordinary times? Like King Henry V, he is, to many, unremarkable, but has survived amid the bloodshed around him. Is he a master politician or has he had good, perhaps exceptional, advice?

Geoff Brock succeeded where other local politicians stumbled or faltered – for example, Labor's Dave McKee, Independent-turned-Labor MP Ted Connelly, eventual Liberal premier John Olsen, and the first Member for Frome, Rob Kerin, also a premier.

Strategists have been savvy enough over the years on the Labor side to realise that having Geoff Brock as an independent candidate for Frome was a brilliant move in terms of potential sympathy for their cause. By also running a Labor candidate, it meant that with the combined vote through Labor preferences, they could thwart the Liberals with an Independent victory.

In 2010, Geoff Brock journeyed to the smelter's gates where the 4 pm siren meant that hordes of workers were finishing their shift. With his supporters, he handed out how-to-vote cards, capitalising on his huge popularity with the union members who are so crucial to the outcome of elections in Port Pirie.

He was liked by the unions. He had the vote of the smelters.

Geoff Brock built on the support he had developed when running for office as councillor and mayor. In 1989 he had amassed an impressive tally of thousands of votes in a council election in which voting was voluntary, gathering more votes than the combined tally of the other five candidates. How many votes could he win in a state election where voting was compulsory?

Just as amazing as his vote-winning strategy, whether devised by himself or others, was his 'clean' image. He travelled with council teams to destinations including Broken Hill where he found it hard to become excited about the two-up games, despite the reactions of his contemporaries. He kept out of trouble, but remained a 'man of the people' who had what one commentator said was the 'gumption' to extract an historic deal from Labor in return for his vote.

Was he a shrewd politician or just a man in the right place at the right time with the right advice?

When this question is put to Geoff Brock, he looks away, pauses and denies receiving any political advice in his campaigns. He says he honed his skills while admiring mayors such as Denis Crisp and Ken Madigan, and Port Pirie Regional Council chief executive officer Ian Burfitt.

'Who have I got to get advice from?' Geoff Brock fires back.

> *No one is going to come forward to help an independent. If you belong to a political party, you have people there to guide you and give advice. When the by-election was called in 2009 – my first state poll – I had only five people I could turn to for advice plus my partner Lyn Akker and what I read in the paper.*

The comparison with King Henry V can be drawn for many independents – unless they do something stupid, they can avoid the decisions that make party politicians unpopular. By keeping his head in the storm, Geoff Brock rose above the traditional approach of blaming political parties for whatever has gone wrong. His supporters would consider him to be a true survivor despite the fluctuating fortunes surrounding his peers. His heart beats as fiercely as the heat from the blast furnace at his beloved smelter. During his time in the smelter's workforce, when leather-bound books of history about the plant were about to be thrown out, Geoff stepped in to claim these irreplaceable records for safekeeping in his home. In the same way, he brokered a deal to save the plant from being consigned to the dustbin of history.

When Geoff Brock travels away from Port Pirie on his parliamentary duties, he can glimpse the towering smelter stack in his car's rear-vision mirror. It may be a fleeting sight, but it represents more than a century of operation and probably another century of survival against the odds for Nyrstar into the future . . . all thanks to the rabbit-trapper's son.

Appendix A

An Excerpt from Geoff Brock's Maiden Speech in State Parliament

[Taken from Hansard 03.03.09]

The SPEAKER: Before I call the member for Frome, I draw the attention of members to the fact that this is his maiden speech to the house, and I ask the house to extend to him the usual courtesies.

Mr BROCK (Frome) (16:03): Thank you, Mr Speaker. As my honourable colleague over here said, I have been a mayor, so I expect a bit of heckling, but I appreciate the protocol of the state parliament. I would just like to commend the bill to the house and, in doing so, I would also like to acknowledge in my maiden speech my colleagues present here today. I have to admit that, being my third sitting week in parliament, I am still finding it a bit daunting. I am still finding my way around the corridors, but I have found where the canteen is and where the toilets are, so that is the main thing.

[*Members interjecting*]

I thought it was quiet, but I will take that as a bit of joviality. I would like to sincerely thank the electors of Frome for voting for me through the democratic process. I assure all the constituents of Frome, and my fellow members here today, that I will do my very best to not only represent them but also work with the elected government, the Opposition and my other parliamentary colleagues within this great institution to ensure that South Australia benefits from all our decisions in this chamber.

I would also like to mention that I am very passionate about regional South Australia in particular, and I would like to work towards regional South Australia's share of resources from this government being recognised and implemented in the future.

Before proceeding, I want to sincerely thank my partner, Lyn, my children and, in particular, our 12 grandchildren for their assistance, their patience and their understanding. It is very hard for them to comprehend the move from being a mayor to the position of a state member of the South Australian parliament. However, as time proceeds, they are becoming more understanding, but they are still a bit concerned that they may not be able to see me as often as previously.

Family is very important to Lyn and I and our children and grandchildren are our priority. This was the reason for becoming involved with local government for the first time 20 years ago and for undertaking the role of mayor of the Port Pirie Regional Council.

Children are our leaders of tomorrow, and we need to do whatever we can to ensure that we all leave a better environment for them. Being an Independent candidate in a by-election was a very daunting experience, indeed. Independent candidates virtually have nowhere to turn to for advice or for resources to manage a campaign.

However, in my case, from nowhere appeared a very small group of passionate volunteers to assist with this campaign. We may be novices, but we learnt as we proceeded, and we had lots of fun learning. At the end of the day, I must admit, the majority of those volunteers had no interest whatsoever in politics but, by the end of the campaign, they were not only interested in politics, but they were very passionate about regional South Australia, and South Australia in particular, and the feeling was one of great achievements.

I sincerely thank the former member, Rob Kerin. Rob carried out his duties as the member for Frome with great passion and dedication. He also carried out the duties of Premier of this great state and leader of the Opposition after the current government came to power. I know the sacrifices that I made as a mayor, let alone the sacrifices Rob has made in his roles over the previous 15 years.

The electorate of Frome – named after E.C. Frome, the third surveyor-general of South Australia – is a very diverse and productive electorate, stretching from the industrial, commercial and retail city of Port Pirie to the agricultural areas of the beautiful township of Clare and the towns of Auburn, Crystal Brook, Gladstone, Georgetown, Laura, Mintaro, Penwortham, Port Broughton, Snowtown, Tarlee and Riverton.

[*Mrs Redmond: 'And Yacka.'*]

And Yacka. You are right, and I apologise for that. It is a diverse electorate, covering more than 7000 square kilometres. I am finding that, over the last three weeks, I have gradually come to grips with all the issues across the whole electorate, covering 4000 kilometres in the past two-and-a-half weeks.

The boundaries have been in place since 1991, and were first contested and won by Rob Kerin in 1993. The largest community within the electorate is Port Pirie where the major employer is the Nyrstar lead and zinc smelter, followed by the Port Pirie Regional Health Service (in the way of numbers of employed people).

With most employment activity within the electorate of Frome being that of price-takers, that is, the prices are dictated by overseas demands, and with what has been happening with the global financial meltdown, it is becoming very hard to manage.

However, knowing the people of Frome, we will persevere and in the finish we will all be stronger for the struggle. While the overheads continue to increase, the final price for the product is diminishing. This is a very daunting thought.

The electorate has been adversely affected by the 'state of Adelaide' attitude, which has seen enormous centralisation over many years. This is still occurring with major moves by the state government. This has not only closed many of our services, but has also resulted in a continuous exodus of many of our youth to Adelaide and elsewhere.

Nowhere has this been more evident than with the long and unpopular implementation of Shared Services which, I must say, has still not been finalised. If this goes ahead in its final form, we will see partners and families of those affected having to relocate from regional South Australia – and Frome is no exception.

This move has a domino effect on associated services, these being reductions in schoolteachers, police and health, to mention a few. These service personnel numbers are based on the number of students and the population of the region concerned (wherever the services may be located).

While there are rural assistance packages for people across the electorate, and South Australia, they are at times very hard to access and understand. Even when they are accessed, the service may not be available due to the fact that it may have been a victim of government rationalisation. I would hope that when this government goes forward it takes these items into consideration.

To try to combat these issues, the regional development boards, namely, the Mid North Regional Development Board at Clare and the Southern Flinders Ranges Development Board at Port Pirie, are working tirelessly to create employment opportunities. The so-called resource boom occurring to the north of the state is a term which I believe has been used for political gain. The only activities occurring are the exploration activities.

Since writing this report, there are a lot of industries feeling the pinch because of the global economic situation. The largest activity is at Roxby Downs, and even they are feeling the pinch, where they are getting ready for the final products, and also the activity at Prominent Hill. There are numerous mining opportunities taking place; however, with the global financial activities and the global uncertainty these projects may not materialise for many years. We just hope that the world comes to its senses and realises that we should all be going forward in a positive manner, not negatively.

Another issue facing any prospect of resource activities continuing is the adequate and guaranteed supply of water to the northern cities, in particular to the northern sector of the state. This issue also confronts other parts of the electorate of Frome, and my fellow members can be assured that I will be working with everyone in this chamber to ensure that this subject is continually in our focus and that we give it the utmost consideration to ensure that not only Frome, but all regional South Australia, and the Eyre Peninsula in particular, has guaranteed water.

Unlike the surrounding areas of Adelaide, these other parts of the state do not have the luxury of having adequate, if any, water catchment facilities to be able to store the water in aquifers or dams.

For this state to prosper, we need to not only focus on the water issue, but also on health issues and facilities across the region, which in the past 12 months have caused great concern and uncertainty in regional South Australia, and I mention the original South Australian Country Health Care Plan that was delivered to communities across regional South Australia.

I do not believe that people living in capital cities realise the importance and appreciate the dependence that country people place on having reliable and easy access to hospital and medical facilities. While another plan came out, the uncertainty is creating issues with the elderly people of our communities. Hospitals are the safety net and, in some locations, the largest providers of employment opportunities, and the uncertainty is causing great stress for the elderly.

I believe communication, clear and precise, is what the communities are looking for, and to be able to have genuine input and suggestions to any changes to both the health system and/or any other facilities that we may have to rationalise or review.

Another area that we as a state do not seem to be focusing enough resources on is education. I know the stimulus package has just come out, however, prior to the global financial meltdown all South Australians were crying out the same message: a lack of skilled labour.

We do not appear to be providing adequate resources and facilities for both education and training opportunities. In particular, in regional parts of South Australia classrooms are becoming crowded and many do not have adequate air-conditioning. I am sure that all members know how uncomfortable it has been with the high temperatures recently and how hard it is to concentrate outside this chamber, once they get out into the open environment.

There is one area which has been of great concern to Port Pirie residents, the region and the state – that is, the image that has been focused on Port Pirie for many years involving high lead levels in the blood of children living in city.

I congratulate this government, in particular Health Minister John Hill and Premier Mike Rann, for their great work and the relationship they have with Nyrstar, the Port Pirie lead smelter and Port Pirie Regional Council. This is a working partnership between the smelter, the council, the Health Department, the Environmental Protection Authority, the whole of state government and, more importantly, the whole community of Port Pirie. The community believes in the project TenBy10 and is getting right behind it. The aim of all the partners is to have 95 per cent of children living in Port Pirie with a lead-in-blood reading below 10 micrograms per decilitre by the end of 2010.

This project has been in place for just over two years and there has been a remarkable reduction in the number of children with reducing lead in blood readings. The local smelter has committed nearly $70 million to environmental improvements, including enclosing the blast furnace of the smelter – something that everyone has been talking about for the past 25 years. I reinforce that this money is to be spent on environmental improvements – nothing extra towards the bottom-line financial gain of the smelter.

The reason for mentioning this is simple. We all have different views both politically and personally, but if we all put aside these differences and work together, we can achieve great results. I know that every member here will put their constituents and South Australia at the top of their priorities and always place them ahead of politics and self.

I have to say that, before entering this house – which I do with great pride – I spent the past 20 years serving the people living in areas surrounding Port Pirie. I did that by sitting on many community committees, far too many to mention. I worked in various positions at the smelter before retiring 18 months ago. I have been an owner-operator of a roadhouse at Port Augusta where I initially employed 15 people and then 45 people after three years. Before that I was a manager for BP Australia at Port Augusta, covering nearly 80 per cent of the northern areas of this great state.

One of the things I have believed throughout the past 20 years, even prior to when I operated the roadhouse and worked at BP Australia, is that working as a team is the only and best way in which to achieve results.

I assure all members and the constituents of Frome that I am here to work with government members and all my other colleagues to ensure that we do the best for this great state and our children and grandchildren.

I thank all members for listening to my maiden speech. I am looking forward to meeting all members in a more informed manner as I go along. I am still learning – and I make no bones about that. I will be sitting here listening. I am not one to jump in. When I do jump in, I will have my facts correct. I want to work with all members on both sides of politics towards a better future for all South Australians.

[*Honourable Members: 'Hear, hear!'*]

Appendix B

Regional Projects

Projects worth many millions of dollars with spin-offs of hundreds of jobs, this is Geoff Brock's answer to his critics. Almost 20 spectacularly successful ventures have risen from the economically challenged South Australian landscape, after being fostered by Geoff's Regional Development Department. Projects range from tomato farms and saltbush production to residential aged care, mushroom plantations and transport hubs.

Some of the ambitious schemes were backed by millions of dollars in government grants.

Listed below with their job outcomes and total private-enterprise investment values, they include:

- Sundrop vegetable industries at Tantanoola: 150 jobs and $80 million investment; at Port Augusta: 200 jobs and $205 million.
- Costa Mushrooms at Monarto: 200 jobs and $65 million.
- Big River Pork at Murray Bridge: 25 jobs and $52 million.
- Mary MacKillop Care SA at Berri: 216 jobs and $16 million.
- Bowmans Intermodal at Bowmans: 15 jobs and $3.9 million.
- Cosmo Glasshouse at Two Wells: 80 jobs and $37 million.
- Days Eggs at Port Germein: 15 jobs and $8 million.
- Lenswood Cold Store at Lenswood: 50 jobs and $12 million.

- Thomas Foods International at Murray Bridge: 200 jobs and $26 million.
- J.T. Johnson at Kapunda: 8 jobs and $3 million.
- Midfield Group at Penola: 35 jobs and $60 million.
- Beston Pure Dairy at Murray Bridge: 61 jobs and $25 million.
- Primo Smallgoods at Port Wakefield: 60 jobs and $5 million.
- Australian Grain at Dublin: 10 jobs and $7 million.
- Chatt Hill Broiler Farm at Murray Bridge: 10 jobs and $9 million.
- Ingham Hatchery at Monarto: 15 jobs and $16 million.
- Wilson Pastoral at Clements Gap: 15 jobs and $1.3 million.
- Liberty House–Onesteel steelworks at Whyalla: 3000 jobs saved and hundreds of millions of dollars in purchase price from United Kingdom group.
- SolarReserve solar-thermal energy project at Port Augusta: 700 jobs and $650 million.

Appendix C

Agreement to Support Stable and Effective Government

The Honourable Jay Weatherill
Member for Cheltenham
Leader of the South Australian Labor Party

and

Mr Geoff Brock
Member for Frome

Agreement to support stable and effective Government

Purpose

1. The State Labor Party has committed to governing for all South Australians.

2. The purpose of this Agreement is to establish stable and effective Government which works productively for all South Australians for the duration of this term of Government.

3. In developing this Agreement, the parties have attempted to, as far as possible, respond to the result of the South Australian State Election held on 15 March 2014.

Acknowledging the independence of the Independent Member

4. In all respects other than as set out in paragraphs 6 to 8, Mr Geoff Brock MP (the **Independent Member**) will vote on bills according to the needs of his electorate and his conscience.

5. Before voting against a bill introduced by the Government, or in favour of a bill introduced by the Opposition, the Independent Member will give the Premier a reasonable opportunity to consult with the Independent Member before the Independent Member votes.

6. The Independent Member will vote with the Government on all appropriation Bills, money Bills and money clauses as defined in the *Constitution Act 1934* (SA).

7. The Independent Member will vote with the Government on all motions of no confidence unless the motion is moved or seconded by the Independent Member, in which case the Independent Member will give the Premier a reasonably opportunity to consult before the Independent Member moves or seconds such a motion.

8. The Independent Member will vote with the Government on all motions to suspend standing orders (including motions to introduce sessional orders) unless the Independent Member gives the Premier a reasonable opportunity to consult with the Independent Member before the Independent Member votes.

Establishing and maintaining a respectful working relationship

9. The Premier will meet with the Independent Member at least once each sitting week, and more often as may be reasonably required by the Independent Member, when Parliament is in session.

10. The Premier (or a designated member of the Cabinet) will meet with the Independent Member (or his delegate) at least once each fortnight when Parliament is not in session.

11. Senior staff members within the Office of the Premier will liaise with staff in the office of the Independent Member to facilitate the meetings referred to in paragraphs 9 and 10, and to ensure that the Independent Member has access to the Premier, Ministers, and key agency officers as may be reasonably required.

12. The Independent Member may at any time, by communicating with the Office of the Premier:

    a. request briefings on Government legislation or policy; and/or

    b. propose policy for consideration by the Government.

13. Upon receiving a communication from an Independent Member in accordance with clause 12(a) above, the Office of the Premier will provide the requested briefing as soon as reasonably practicable.

14. Upon receiving a communication from an Independent Member in accordance with clause 12(b) above, the Office of the Premier will arrange for an advice on the proposal (including advice on the budgetary implications of the proposal) to be provided to the Independent Member as soon as reasonably practicable.

15. The obligations set out in clauses 10 to 14 above may be amended by agreement between the Premier and the Independent Member.

Responding to the State Election

Increased transparency of election costings

16. During the 2014 State Election, both major parties criticised the costings approach of the other major party. The Government and the Independent Member will work together to establish a process whereby:

    a. political parties may submit policies to a Parliamentary Budget Advisory Service (**PBAS**) for costing in the period leading up to and including the election;

    b. in the event that a political party declines to submit any policy for costing to the PBAS, that fact will be required to be revealed on the release of that policy, and in material referring to that policy;

    c. a list of the policies submitted by the political parties to the PBAS will be published by the PBAS four days prior to election day to enable proper scrutiny of the parties' costings;

d. except for the publication under paragraph 16(c) above, advice provided to or from the PBAS will remain confidential to the party submitting the relevant policy.

Election Conduct

17. During the State Election, there were instances of conduct by candidates and political parties which were not in accordance with the *Electoral Act 1985*, and which were not corrected during the election period.

18. The Government will work together with the Independent Member and the Parliament to establish a Select Committee to inquire into and report on the parts of the *Electoral Act 1985* governing the conduct of parties and candidates in elections, and in particular the parts governing the enforcement of rulings by the Electoral Commissioner, in the context of the 2014 State Election.

Parliamentary Conduct

19. The Government and the Independent Member agree that there is a justified concern in the community about the standards of parliamentary conduct.

20. The Government will work together with the Independent Member and the Parliament to introduce a code of conduct for members of Parliament.

Regional South Australia

21. The Government and the Independent Member agree that the election result indicates that the Government must re-establish confidence in regional communities that their concerns are effectively heard within Government and are responded to.

22. The Government and the Independent Member will work together to establish a charter to ensure that the needs and special circumstances of regional South Australia are taken into account by the Government when developing legislation and policy, and in particular, to ensure that regional South Australia benefits from economic development and receives fair access to Government services.

Small Business

23. The Government and the Independent Member agree that the election result indicates that the Government must re-establish confidence in the small business community that its concerns are effectively heard within Government and are responded to.

24. The Government and the Independent Member will work together to establish a charter to ensure that the needs and special circumstances of small business are taken into account by the Government when developing legislation and policy.

General

25. The parties acknowledge that this Agreement represents their understanding and intentions but that neither party is constrained from acting in what they consider to be the best interests of the State of South Australia. However, the parties undertake that, in so far as it is consistent with their duty, before taking any action to bring this

Agreement to an end, that party will communicate with the other parties with a view to reaching an accommodation consistent with the intent and purpose of this Agreement.

26. This Agreement will come into effect upon the execution of this Agreement by the parties.

Signed this 22nd day of March 2014

The Honourable Jay Weatherill
Member for Cheltenham
Leader of the South Australian Labor Party

Mr Geoff Brock
Member for Frome

Appendix D

Weatherill/Brock Agreement

The Honourable Jay Weatherill
Member for Cheltenham
Leader of the South Australian Labor Party
("Premier")

and

Mr Geoff Brock
Member for Frome
("Minister")

Agreement

(A) The Premier leads a Labor Government, after the State Election held on 15 March 2014, and is in a position to form a minority Government.

(B) The Premier and the Minister agree that it is in the best interests of the people of South Australia that the Minister be appointed as a minister within the Labor Government.

(C) The Minister is neither a member of the Labor Party nor the Liberal Party ("the major parties") and will remain unaffiliated with the major parties.

(D) The purpose of this Agreement is to record the political understanding reached between the Premier and the Minister as to how the Minister can be a member of the Labor Government whilst remaining unaffiliated with the major parties.

(E) The Premier and the Minister agree that the Minister will have a special position in Cabinet in that, by reason of his non-affiliation with the Labor Party, there is a class of issues in respect of which it will not always be possible for the Minister to be bound by a Cabinet decision (the class is defined in clause 3 and are referred to in this Agreement as "**Issues**"). The agreement reached between the Premier and the Minister is intended to reduce to a minimum any matters where the Minister will not be able to agree to a decision of Cabinet, but acknowledges that when such a circumstance arises, the parties will seek to identify it as early as possible and the Minister will absent himself from the Cabinet discussion at the earliest time.

1. **APPOINTMENT AS PORTFOLIO MINISTER**

In the event that the Premier is able to form a minority government, the Premier will advise His Excellency the Governor to appoint the Minister to a ministerial portfolio to be determined by the Premier.

1.1 The Minister will have authority to enter into contracts on behalf of the State for the purposes of his portfolio.

1.2 In each of his Ministerial capacities, the Minister will be serviced by and may give directions to the Departments to which his ministerial capacities relate in accordance with the *Public Sector Act, 2010*.

1.3 The Premier will, at the request of the Minister, engage personal staff selected by the Minister, in consultation with the Premier, to assist the Minister.

1.4 In performing his portfolio responsibilities the Minister must give effect to (in order of priority):

1.4.1 Any applicable laws or directions, instructions or orders having legal effect;

1.4.2 Any decisions of the Executive Council;

1.4.3 Any decisions of Cabinet;

1.4.4 Any policies agreed between the Minister and the Premier;

1.4.5 Save as specified in para 2.7 of the Agreement, any relevant policies announced by the Labor Party in the 2014 South Australian election ("Labor Policies").

1.5 Where the Minister is unable or unwilling to perform his Ministerial responsibilities in accordance with 2.4, the Minister must immediately inform the Premier of that fact, together with his reasons, and will meet with the Premier as soon as may be convenient in order to seek some accommodation between them.

1.6 The Minister must make every effort to provide the Premier with as much notice as possible when the Minister is unwilling or unable to perform his Ministerial responsibilities in accordance with 2.4.

1.7 It is understood that the Minister may not have to comply with Labor policies in relation to:

1.7.1 significant matters affecting the small business and regional communities; and

1.7.2 issues believed to be matters of conscience.

1.8 The Minister will be bound by the Ministerial Code of Conduct except as provided for in this Agreement.

2. ATTENDANCE AT CABINET

2.1 The Minister will be provided the same Cabinet papers as every other Minister.

2.2 The Minister will peruse those Cabinet documents at his earliest opportunity.

2.3 If, after reading a Cabinet document, in the opinion of the Minister, it would be inconsistent with the Minister's non-affiliation with the major parties for the Minister to be bound by a Cabinet decision in relation to an Issue, the Minister must immediately upon reaching that opinion, inform the Premier of that fact, together with his reasons, and will meet with the Premier as soon as may be convenient in order to seek some accommodation between them in relation to the policy and/or procedure to be followed.

2.4 The Minister must make every effort to provide the Premier with as much notice as possible when the Minister believes a matter for decision in Cabinet will be inconsistent with the Minister's non-affiliation with the major parties.

2.5 The Minister agrees that in this Agreement, the Issues will be limited to:

2.5.1 issues with direct and immediate effect upon the Minister's electorate;

2.5.2 significant matters affecting the small business and regional communities;

2.5.3 such other matters as the Minister has advised the Premier from time to time in writing.

2.6 If, after the meeting referred to in clause 3.3 of this Agreement, no other accommodation can be reached then the Minister will:

2.6.1 immediately return to the Cabinet office all copies of the relevant Cabinet documents and all notes or other records relating to the relevant Cabinet documents or copies; and

2.6.2 absent himself from that part of the Cabinet discussion where the relevant matter will be or is being discussed.

2.7 Even where the Minister has absented himself from Cabinet in accordance with this clause, the Minister agrees that he will not criticise, comment or or disclose the relevant policy until the policy has been publicly announced by the Government.

2.8 The Premier agrees that the Minister, having complied with the arrangements in this Agreement, is not subject to the usual rules of Cabinet solidarity in respect of that particular matter. In particular, the Minister, whilst remaining a member of the Cabinet, may criticise the particular Government policy in relation to which the Minister absented himself from Cabinet after the policy has been publicly announced.

2.9 The Minister may not divulge any of the material in any Cabinet documents and is bound by Cabinet secrecy in the same way as any Minister notwithstanding, anything in this Agreement.

2.10 Except as provided in this Agreement:

(a) The Minister will be a full member of Cabinet with the same entitlements to take matters to Cabinet, to discuss matters within Cabinet and to vote on matters in Cabinet as any other Minister.

(b) The Minister will be subject to the usual rules of Cabinet solidarity.

3. EXECUTIVE COUNCIL

3.1 The Minister agrees that he will not provide advice directly to the Governor except with the prior approval of the Premier.

3.2 The Minister agrees that he will not attend an Executive Council meeting where there is on the agenda a matter upon which he absented himself from Cabinet in accordance with clause 3 of this Agreement.

5 VOTING IN PARLIAMENT

5.1 Save for a matter on which the Minister has absented himself from Cabinet in accordance with clause 3 of the Agreement, the Minister agrees to support the Government in the Parliament and to vote with the Government on any matter raised in the Parliament which has received the prior approval of Cabinet.

5.2 The Minister is not obliged to support the Government in the Parliament nor to vote with the Government in relation to:

5.2.1 matters about which he has absented himself from Cabinet or

5.2.2 votes concerning Issues about which he has given notice to the Premier (unless he has voted in Cabinet in relation to that Issue).

5.3 The obligation on the Minister to vote to support the Government in the circumstances set out in clause 5.1 above, is in addition to any other obligations the Minister has entered into with the Government regarding support for the Government on matters of appropriation, money bills and clauses, and confidence.

6. EFFECT OF AGREEMENT

The parties acknowledge that this Agreement represents their understanding and intentions, but that neither party is thereby constrained from acting in what they perceive to be the best interests of the State of South Australia. However, both parties undertake, so far as is consistent with their duty, that before taking any action to bring this Agreement to an end that party will communicate with the other with a view to reaching some accommodation consistent with the intent and purpose of this Agreement.

....

Hon Jay Weatherill
Member for Cheltenham
Leader of the South Australian Labor Party

22 March 2014

....

Geoff Brock
Member for Frome
22nd March 2014.

Index

S

T

V

W

X

Z

Wakefield Press is an independent publishing and distribution company based in Adelaide, South Australia. We love good stories and publish beautiful books. To see our full range of books, please visit our website at wakefieldpress.com.au where all titles are available for purchase. To keep up with our latest releases, news and events, subscribe to our monthly newsletter.

Find us!

Facebook: facebook.com/wakefield.press
Twitter: twitter.com/wakefieldpress
Instagram: instagram.com/wakefieldpress

Printed in Australia
AUOW01n1646120118
293541AU00001B/1

9 781743 0552